SpringerBriefs in Well-Being and Quality of Life Research

More information about this series at http://www.springer.com/series/10150

G.K. Lieten · Talinay Strehl

Child Street Life

An Inside View of Hazards and Expectations of Street Children in Peru

Springer

G.K. Lieten
Heemstede
The Netherlands

Talinay Strehl
Amsterdam
The Netherlands

ISSN 2211-7644 ISSN 2211-7652 (electronic)
ISBN 978-3-319-11721-8 ISBN 978-3-319-11722-5 (eBook)
DOI 10.1007/978-3-319-11722-5

Library of Congress Control Number: 2014950523

Springer Cham Heidelberg New York Dordrecht London

Printed on acid-free paper

Springer is part of Springer Science+Business Media (www.springer.com)

Preface

Social phenomena are subject to trends, hypes and fashion. During the last two decades of the previous century, the street child phenomenon was subject to academic and policy attention, for very good reasons, namely numerous children living and working in the street.

Although the problem remains as serious a social problem as before, public attention appears to have shifted to other social issues. Fewer studies have been conducted and the direct redressal appears to have taken backstage. There namely has been a paradigmatic shift: presently, in most academic studies, the street child is iconized as a social agent, with a free will and with autonomous choices of survival.

This publication is a reminder of a loathsome condition of human existence of street life in two cities in Latin America. It gives voice to the children and, in the process, realizes that there is a strong argument in favour of the traditional policies of protection rather than for the fashionable 'agency' approach which today dominates the literature on child rights.

The uniqueness of this study is the combination of a large-scale sociological survey with in-depth anthropological fieldwork. Around 1,100 street children have been interviewed in two major cities in Peru. We thank them for their cooperation and trust. For reasons of privacy, their names have been altered. We believe that a better understanding of their position will eventually lead to better policies.

Since we have taken extreme care to listen to the stories of as many children as possible and to let them speak through the pages of this book, this publication will be extremely useful for anybody working with children in such dismal conditions as street life, not only in Peru or Latin America.

Contents

Chapter 1
Victims and Agents

> Being poor is itself a health hazard; worse, however, is being urban and poor. Much worse is being poor, urban and a child. But worst of all is being a street child in an urban environment (De la Barra 1998: 46).

A phenomenon characterising urban areas in developing countries all over the world is the presence of deprived children who depend on the streets for their survival, the so-called 'street children'. Usually they are dispossessed of almost all the rights embodied in the United Nation Convention on the Rights of the Child of 1989. As Ennew (1995) has stated in her seminal study, street children are 'society's ultimate outlaws', who are 'not only outside society, they are also outside childhood'.

Reliable data on how many children work or live on the streets worldwide are not available. UNICEF (2002: 37) and other UN sources have estimated the number of street children to be possibly as high as 150 million, of which 25 million in Latin America. As population growth and urbanisation continue, and social inequity endures, these numbers are expected to be increasing (UNICEF 2005: 40–41). However, important features of this sector, particularly its footloose character and its heterogeneous composition, contribute to the lack of unpolluted statistics. The estimates, as some have argued, have a function as advocacy statistics, which 'are produced to draw attention to the need for the agency's work. At best, these estimates rest upon largely elastic and nebulous definitions of homeless and working children' (Ennew 2000: 170, 2003). Although this reading has some validity, the phenomenon of street children, whatsoever the figures, is a glaringly observable social problem. A good summary can be found in a recent report of the High Commissioner for Human Rights:

> It is not known how many children depend on the streets for their survival or development. Numbers fluctuate according to socio-economic, political and cultural conditions, including growing urbanization and inequalities, as well as terminology and definitions used. What is known is that diverse conditions and multiple rights violations push children

G.K. Lieten and T. Strehl, *Child Street Life*, SpringerBriefs in Well-Being and Quality of Life Research 15, DOI 10.1007/978-3-319-11722-5_1

> into developing connections with the streets. Once there, children face a range of new challenges, including hostile perceptions of them as delinquents, and many forms of violence (UNHR 2012: 20).

This monograph will study the phenomenon of street children in two cities in Peru. It will look at some of the conceptual issues and, after analysing why children are in the street and what behaviour and which aspirations they exhibit, will deal with the policy issues and lessons to be learned.

While doing the field work, we have adopted a child-centred approach. A central objective is to reveal the faces and voices of street children and analyse their relationship with the street and their perceptions of their situation. We want to understand their coping mechanisms, and their (self-declared) needs and their (perceived) aspirations. Useful research tools, in addition to the quantitative survey and the many individual testimonies, were participative photography[1] and the 'ranking game': children were asked to put cards representing different images in order of appreciation or importance. The cards showed images of street life, work, problems, aspirations, street child services, and other issues in their lives.

The broad classification 'street children' is imperfect and leads to misunderstandings and inefficient policy. The street child as a sign of school exclusion and as a runaway place of degenerative estrangement refers only to the category of totally abandoned children (Williams 1993). It is a minority. Most of the so-called street-children fluidly move on and off the streets and are embedded in a social network. Many of them in fact live with their families, go to school and hang around or work on the streets for a couple of hours per day. Because the overall term is insensitive to the differences among all the children that it attempts to categorise,[2] UNICEF has introduced the distinction between children *on* the street and children *of* the street. This categorisation is based on the level of contact the children have with their families. The first category (*on* the streets) consists of children who take to the streets for a livelihood, but who return home to their families and contribute to the household income; the latter (*of* the streets) refers to children without family support and who have come to depend entirely on the streets for survival (usually run-away children). Another distinction is that between 'street-working children' and 'street-living children' (Consortium 1999). This definition is actually more in line with the formulation of UNICEF in the 1990s, when on the basis of the distinction made by Jo Boyden the formulation 'street and working children' was adopted (Black 1993).

---

[1] In both Lima and Cusco, photography workshops with disposable cameras were organised at two open street child shelters. In total, 20 street-living children participated. They were asked to photograph their daily lives on the street, especially things they do and don't like about street life. Afterwards the photos were discussed with the children individually in the form of semi-structured interviews.

[2] Children working on the streets but living at home, children helping family members on the street, children working at markets, children living with family on the street, children sleeping in night shelters, children without any family contact, children sleeping temporarily or permanently on the streets, children in youth gangs, etc.

Admittedly, the group boundaries are fluid. This divergence in the past has officially been recognised as a basis for policy (UNICEF 1986). It was considered appropriate to distinguish the numerous children who in developing countries, for various reasons, are spending much of their time in the streets, from those children who literally live in the streets. In many rather recent anthropological studies, this distinction is considered as unimportant. The very terminology of street children is rejected with the argument that it is all-inclusive. Presently, in a new paradigm, the term 'street children' tends to be categorized as being a 'social construction'. Panter-Brick (2002: 150), in line with many other anthropologists, had actually argued that 'the focus on discrete categories of street lifestyles has fallen into disuse' and therefore needs to be replaced by a better concept (see also Thomas de Benitez 2007; UNHR 2012).[3] The alternative terminology, which has gained currency—'children with street connection'—it seems, actually suffers even more from the weaknesses in the rejected terminology: it is all-inclusive, multidimensional and purely descriptive.

A number of anthropologists similarly argue that the term 'street children' is a stigmatising label, and therefore 'inappropriate, offensive and gives an excluded message' (Dallape 1988, quoted in Ennew 2003: 7). In many such studies, the street child is even eulogised with the argument that the child had developed agency and has found imaginative ways of surviving in the urban jungle. It is appreciated for its resilience and ingenuity in coping with difficult circumstances. Morrow and Richards (1996: 90) argue that the portrayal of children as vulnerable, incompetent and relatively powerless in society is deeply problematic and that they rather should be seen as agents of change. Concepts like agency, resilience and coping with adversity are instrumental in emphasizing 'children's rights as citizens and (it) recognizes their capabilities to enact change in their own lives' (Panter-Brick 2002: 147; see also similar arguments in Aptekar 1988, 1991; Glauser 1990; Lucchini 1997; Hecht 1998; Invernizzi 2003; Ennew 2003; Gigengack 2006).

There are two opposing schools of thought: the *regulacionistas* and the *abolicionistas*.[4] The majority of child centred NGOs that work with street-working or

---

[3] The rejection of analytical distinctions is defended with the argument that street children do not form a clearly defined, homogeneous population (this argument, we feel, may be valid for any analytical category), but instead refer to a subject constructed through discourse and thus may be captured by any number of definitions, dependent on the dimension of street life that is focused upon (see also de Benitez 2011: 8; Nikitina-Den Besten 2008 for a synopsis of the new child paradigm, based on agency and the social construction of categories).

[4] Literally: those who want to regulate child labour and those who want to abolish it. The former believe that children should have the right to work and that work is a part of life in many cultures. According to them, the focus should be on improving working conditions instead of eliminating all forms of child labour, which is exactly what the latter propose (see e.g. Liebel 2004; Weston 2005; Bourdillon et al. 2010; they reject the distinction between working children and child labour and regard the latter as a pejorative stigmatisation). The latter approach, replacing a specific analytical category ('child labour') by a general and descriptive category ('working child') has found many followers, particularly in the NGO world. For a critical assessment of their theory in practice, see Van den Berge (2007).

street-living children in Peru are also somehow involved in this controversy. The *abolicionista* stance is supported by the ILO, UNICEF and the Peruvian state. The *regulacionista* (agency) position is taken by many internationally-operating NGO's. Whereas the *abolicionistas* take a more protectionist stance in which adults decide what is best for the children (and oppose 'child labour' and of-the-street children), the *regulacionistas* defend the rights of 'working children'. They treat children as 'social subjects with the capacity to participate in society and to transform it' (Liebel 2004), and thus also to participate in street life on adult terms.

We shall argue otherwise. The typologies have an analytical validity. They help to distinguish the difference between 'agency' and 'victim' and between what is despicable and what may help in the development of the child.[5] The typologies are not meant to neatly classify all street children within discrete categories but are meant as an analytical category, which helps us in understanding different forms of street life. A standard definition, provided by the UN, refers to 'boys and girls for whom 'the street' (including unoccupied dwellings, wasteland, etc.) has become their home and/or source of livelihood, and who are inadequately protected or supervised by responsible adults' (quoted in Volpi 2002: 2–3). The advantage of this definition is that it also includes children staying at home but who are 'inadequately protected or supervised' while spending much of their time in the street.

The various categories of children are interconnected. It is 'flows' rather than 'stocks' (Volpi 2002: 5): children move in and out of subcategories. This monograph shall investigate when and why the transition from children on the street (street-working children) to children of the street (street living children) takes place and to elucidate how they survive. It thus helps to explain the fluidity and the risks involved in any type of child street life.

References

Aptekar, L. (1988). *Street children of Cali*. Durham: Duke University Press.

Aptekar, L. (1991). Are Columbian street children neglected? *Anthropology of education, 22*, 326–349.

Black, M. (1993). *Street and working children. Innocenti global seminar. Summary report*. Florence: Innocenti.

[5] We regard agency of street children as a subsidiary activity, imposed upon the child by developments and circumstances outside its autonomy. It is an agency prompted by an iniquitous system. By following the life track of the individual child, from a place within an impoverished and crisis-ridden family to the livelihood as a child of the street, we have clarified the subsidiary nature of their agency, the agency of the marginalized and unprotected. On the contrary, the abstraction of agency, isolating it from the material circumstances, is typical for the functionalist school in sociology, which focuses on personal traits and social functioning rather than on social conditioning.

Bourdillon, M., Levison, D., Myers, W., & White, B. (2010). *Rights and wrongs of children's work.* London: Rutgers University Press.
Consortium for Street Children. (1999). *Prevention of street migration.* London: Consortium for Street Children.
Dallape, F. (1988). *An experience with street children.* Nairobi: Undugu Society.
de Benitez, S. T. (2007). *State of the world's street children: Violence.* London: Consortium of Street Children.
de Benitez, S. T. (2011). *State of the world's street children: Research.* London: Consortium of Street Children.
De la Barra, X. (1998). Poverty: The main cause of ill health in urban children. *Health Education Behavior, 25*(1), 45–49.
Ennew, J. (1995). Outside childhood. Street children's rights. In B. Franklin (Ed.). *The handbook of children's rights.* London: Routledge.
Ennew, J. (2000). Why the convention is not about street children. In D. Fottrell (Ed.), *Revisiting children's rights: 10 years of the UN convention on the rights of the child.* The Hague: Kluwer Law International.
Ennew, J. (2003). Difficult circumstances: some reflections on street children in Africa. *Children, Youth and Environment, 13*(1), 128–146.
Gigengack, R. (2006). *Young, damned and banda. The world of young street people in Mexico City, 1990–1997.* Amsterdam: Amsterdam School for Social Science Research.
Glauser, B. (1990). Street children: deconstructing a construct. In A. James & A. Prout (Eds.), *Constructing and reconstructing childhood: contemporary issues in the sociological study of childhood.* London: Palmer Press.
Hecht, T. (1998). *At home in the street. Street children of Northeast Brazil.* Cambridge: University Press.
Invernizzi, A. (2003). Street-working children and adolescents in Lima: Work as an agent of socialization. *Childhood, 10*, 319–341.
Liebel, M. (2004). *A will of their own. Cross-cultural perspectives on working children.* London: Zed Books.
Lucchini, R. (1997). *Deviance and street children in Latin America: The limits of a functionalist approach.* Fribourg: The University of Fribourg Press.
Morrow, F. & Richards, M. (1996). The ethics of social research with children: an overview. *Children and Society, 10*, 90–105.
Nikitina-Den Besten ON (2008) What's new in the new social studies of childhood? The changing meaning of "childhood". *Social Sciences*, October, available at http://ssrn.com/abstract=1285085
Panter-Brick, C. (2002). Street children, human rights, and public health: A critique and future directions. *Annual Review of Anthropology, 31*, 147–171.
UNICEF. (1986). *Exploitation of working children and street children.* New York: UNICEF Executive Board. (1986 session, E/ICEF/1986/CRP.3).
UNICEF. (2002). *The state of the world's children 2003: Child participation.* New York: UNICEF.
UNICEF. (2005). *The state of the world's children 2006: Excluded and invisible.* New York: The United Nations Children's Fund.
United Nations. (1989). *Convention on the rights of the child.* Available in http://www.hrweb.org/legal/child.html; http://www.unhchr.ch/html/menu3/b/k2crc.htm
UNHR. (2012). *Protection and promotion of the rights of children working and/or living on the street.* Geneva: OHCHR.
Van den Berge, M. (2007). *Working children's organisations in Peru.* Amsterdam: IREWOC.
Volpi, E. (2002). *Street children. Promising practices and approaches.* Washington: The World Bank Working Papers (26388).
Weston, B. (Ed.). (2005). *Child labor and human rights.* Boulder: Lynne Reiner.
Williams, C. (1993). Who are "street children"? A hierarchy of street use and appropriate responses. *Child Abuse and Neglect, 17*, 831–841.

Chapter 2
Research and Overview

The data presented in this monograph are the result of several successive anthropological and sociological fieldwork periods with a child-centred approach in Lima and Cusco. Being a street-living child is a phenomenon at a given moment in time. Some children only know the street as their habitat, but most children indeed experience a constant flux in their lives between street and home. The common trait is poverty, mobility and disturbed family structures.

Children growing up in Peru are among Latin America's most deprived population. According to UNICEF, one out of every four young children live in circumstances that can be labelled as extreme poverty (UNICEF 2008: 2). The country has witnessed a rapid growth of its urban areas due to massive migration from the rural areas. Three fourth of the population is urban; slums and the informal sector have grown excessively (Valenzuela et al. 2007: 35; Velazco 2004; Espinoza and Rios 2006: 9–11). People flock to the cities in search of a better life. Lima, presently with close to 10 million inhabitants, embodies this trend. So does the Andean mountain town of Cusco, with rapidly expanding outskirts with migrants from the countryside in search of work. This 'archaeological capital of America', close to Machhu Pichu, and thus a tourist hub, annually receives more tourists than there are residents but still an estimated 75 % of the inhabitants live below the poverty line (Steel 2008: 47).

The data presented in this monograph are the result of several successive anthropological and sociological fieldwork periods in these two cities in Peru: Lima and Cusco. It is based on altogether 5 months on the streets and in street child shelters and it documents the views and opinions of the children, their families/caretakers and extension workers. It was important to first establish trust with a number of these children on the street and the places they hang out, such as the beach, illegal hostels, pinball halls and internet cafés. These 'gatekeepers' introduced us to their friends on the street. Once initial contacts had been established, we started with a quantitative study.

G.K. Lieten and T. Strehl, *Child Street Life*, SpringerBriefs in Well-Being and Quality of Life Research 15, DOI 10.1007/978-3-319-11722-5_2

In Lima, 12 enquirers collected questionnaires from among 827 street-working and street-living children, aged between 5 and 17, in different parts of the city. In Cusco, 6 enquirers collected questionnaires from among a total of 341 street-working and street-living children. Around one third of the questionnaires were recorded late in the evening or at night.

The field workers responsible for approaching and interviewing the children were all Peruvians living in Lima and Cusco. Most of them had experience in working with street children or working children. Consecutively, after initial analysis of the data had been conducted, anthropological field work started. Participant observation of the streets was remarkably easier in Cusco than in Lima, due to the dangerous character of specific areas in the latter city and the more extreme marginalisation of street children. Individual and group interviews were conducted with many children; sometimes these were spontaneous and sometimes planned. While some of the children preferred to be interviewed alone, others were more talkative when their friends were around. In total, 42 semi-formal interviews were conducted, with 30 boys and 12 girls. A lot of relevant data, however, was gathered during the dozens of informal talks.

We have to keep in mind, as said earlier, that 'children move fluidly on and off the streets and that the street does not represent the sum total of their social networks and experiences' (Panter-Brick 2002: 148). Being a street-living child is a phenomenon at a given moment in time. Some children only know the street as their habitat, but most children indeed experience a constant flux in their lives between street and home. They, for instance, have regular contact with their parents or occasionally return home. Actually, it was a challenge to find children who entirely and at all times fits the category of street-living children, because regular changes in lifestyles and activities is what characterises them specifically. The street-living children in this research shared the specific characteristic of not living in their home, and living on the street at that given moment.

The survey resulted in data on around 200 children in Lima and 50 children in Cusco who answered to the definition of street-living children. At the time of the research, they lived in a shelter, rented room, outside, in parks, on the streets or in dilapidated buildings. Most of the other children (the street-working children) spent the night at the family home. If they stay with one parent, it usually is a mother-headed family. Among the children sleeping in the open air or in dilapidated buildings, we counted only 5 girls and no child younger than 10 years (Table 2.1).

It is hard to aggregate these numbers, statistically, into the total number of street-living children, since only a selection of neighbourhoods was included in the survey and because children *of* the street are generally harder to contact than children *working on* the street. Comparing this number with a census done in 2008 by street educators in Lima (Voces para Latinoamérica and Sinergia por la Infancia 2009), together with our qualitative observations and information from street workers, we estimate the number of street-living children in Lima to be probably less than 1,000 (Ordóñez 1995: 75; Vara Horna 2002; Tejada Ripalda 2005: 37;

Table 2.1 Usual sleeping place of all street children in both cities

	Total	Percentage (%)
Both parents	436	37.2
One single parent	329	28.1
Other family members	136	11.6
Hostel/dormitory/rented place	169	14.4
Open air	37	3.2
Deserted building	8	0.7
Hogar children's home	13	1.1
Otherwise	8	0.7
No response	35	3.0
	1,171	100

Source IREWOC (2012), Tablas Estadísticas—Niños y Niñas de la calle en Lima y Cusco (Table 4)

Voces 2009). Based on observations in our study, we estimate the number of street-living children in Cusco to be around 100.[1]

Most street-working and street-living children come from poor families, usually either first or second generation migrants. Sometimes the children themselves are first generation migrants and still have parents living in the countryside. In Lima, although 57 % of the interviewed children were born in the city, a significant number (29 %) was born in la Sierra, the central highlands of Peru, which includes also the poorest departments of Peru; the rest was born in the coastal area and in the Amazon region. They had migrated fairly recently. At the moment of the survey, one fifth of all children had their mother living outside Lima. In Cusco, 40 % had migrated to Cusco recently, either alone or with their parents. In Cusco, like in Lima, a quarter of the children lived without a mother and even one third lived without a father. There thus appeared to be a strong correlation between dysfunctional and broken families and the need for a child to work on the streets: more than half of all the street-working children in the sociological survey (62 % in Lima and 53 % in Cusco) did not have a complete nuclear family.

In Lima, many more boys than girls are working or living on the streets, respectively 63 and 37 % (see also Table 2.2 for general information on numbers). The gender difference hardly applies to the younger categories: among the youngest children, girls are even in the majority. The gender difference is marked in the age category 14–17. In this cohort, there are twice as many boys as girls. Within the

[1] Other studies, done by NGO's, have higher estimates. A study done in Cusco in 1996 by the NGO ensing Maki estimated a number of 3,130 street-working children between 6 and 17 years old (Baufumé and Astete 1998). In 2009 Cusco's night shelter for street children, Qosqo Maki, received 179 individual children, ranging from 5 to 17 years old. This gives an indication of the number of children living in the street in Cusco. However, most of these children stayed only for a short time, or at intervals. This shows the fluidity of the street child population.

Table 2.2 Gender/age of all street children enumerated in Cusco and Lima

Age	Girls	Boys	Lima	Cusco
5–9	94	87	122	59
10–13	164	172	295	141
14–17	199	352	410	141
Total	457	611	827	341

Source IREWOC (2012), Tablas Estadísticas—Niños y Niñas de la calle en Lima y Cusco (seccion 1)

population of street-living children proper the gender difference is bigger: 89 % are boys, while just 11 % are girls. Compared to Lima, the difference between the number of boys and girls working on Cusco's streets is relatively small, but within the population of street-living children this difference was bigger: 82 % were boys and 18 % girls. Girls thus are still a minority, both *on* the street and *in* the street. One of the explanations is that girls are more resilient than boys and may cope with problems at home for a longer time, even when they are abused or maltreated. Besides, girls generally may feel more emotionally connected to family members and feel more responsible to help. Also, even after girls leave home, they generally find family contact more important than boys do and may find distant family members to live with. Girls are expected to stay at home with their parents, in the private space, while the streets are an already accepted domain for boys. Lancy (2010) argues that street kids are more likely to be male, because girls are both more useful and valued at home and, simultaneously more vulnerable and likely to become 'damaged' in the street. The street girl's vulnerability for dangers such as sexual abuse and violence is possibly one of the reasons why more girls than boys are afraid to walk away from the (reasonably safe) home environment. In the case of extreme problems at home more girls opt for a life in a children's or girls' home instead of the street. An additional explanation for the low number of street girls in Cusco could be their 'invisibility' on the streets, for example, because of their employment in more hidden sectors like prostitution in brothels or their living with a 'sugar daddy' (Steel 2008: 72; Woan et al. 2013: 3) (Table 2.2).

References

Baufumé, I. R., & Astete, J. V. (1998). *Trabajando en las calles de mi ciudad*. Cusco: Asociación Qosqo Maki.

Espinoza, H., & Rios, V. (2006). *Mecanismos de protección social de salud en el sector informal urbano del Perú*. Lima: CEDEP, CIES.

IREWOC. (2012). *Tablas Estadísticas—Niños y Niñas de la calle en Lima y Cusco*. Leiden: IREWOC.

Lancy, D. F. (2010). *The Anthropology of Learning in Childhood*. Walnut Creek: AltaMira Press.

Ordóñez, D. (1995). *Niños de la calle y sus familias en Lima: una realidad en 852 variables*. Lima: Ed. Ayni/Opcion.

Panter-Brick, C. (2002). Street children, human rights, and public health: A critique and future directions. *Annual Review of Anthropology, 31*, 147–171.

Steel, G. (2008). *Vulnerable careers. Tourism and livelihood dynamics among street vendors in Cusco, Peru*. Amsterdam: Rozenberg Publishers.

Tejada Ripalda, L. (2005). *Los niños de la calle y su mundo*. Lima: Fondo Editorial de la Facultad de Ciencias Sociales, Universidad Nacional de San Marcos.

UNICEF. (2008). *Situation of children in Peru. Executive summary*. Lima: UNICEF. (http://www.unicef.org/peru/spanish/Folleto_ing_correc_1.pdf).

Valenzuela, J., et al. (2007). *Unidos Sí Podemos*. Lima: Cesip, Ceprodep, Cordaid.

Vara Horna, A. A. (2002). *Primer Censo de los niños de la calle*. Available from http://www.aristidesvara.com/investigaciones/psicologia/informe_estadistico/censo_20.htm.

Velazco, J. (2004). *La Protección Social para Trabajadores Informales en el Perú: Estimación de su cobertura a partir de la ENAHO-2002*. Lima: Consorcio de Investigación Económica y Social (CIES), WIEGO y (PUCP).

Voces para Latinoamérica., & Sinergia por la Infancia. (2009). *Perfil de Niños-as y Adolescentes en Situacion de Calle (Inhaladores), Lima (Perú)*. Lima: Voces para Latinoamérica.

Woan, J., Lin, J., & Auerswald, C. (2013). The health status of street children and youth in low- and middle-income countries: A systematic review of the literature. *Journal of Adolescent Health, 30*, 1–8.

Chapter 3
Landing in the Streets: A Multiplicity of Factors

The *callejización* (street migration) consists of different stages of decision-making in which the child becomes more and more alienated from home and in which the family contacts diminish. Pull and push forces need to be treated separately.

The social norm across cultures is that children, well into the age of adolescence, live with their parents or guardians, or, in any case, with adults whose responsibility it is, to the extent possible, to look after the material need and to educate them, socially, morally and intellectually. When such a protective shelter fails, and children have to fence on their own, living and sleeping rough, a complexity of reasons is likely to be in place. We shall look at these various mechanisms to which the children succumb and which basically integrate into a many-fold cluster of poverty.

3.1 Family Circumstances

Due to a lack of infrastructure and housing space for the fast growing population, many migrants from the countryside have settled down in the city outskirts where they have constructed illegal squatter settlements, the so-called *barriadas*, which later have grown into residential communities, called *pueblos jovenes*. Housing conditions in these localities are usually cramped and, even in comparison with the street, not a comfortable place to live in.

The average number of children per family was 5 in Lima and 4 in Cusco. Some children, however, come from families with up to 12 brothers and sisters. Here we should keep in mind that, as a result of broken families, and rebuilt families, many children have half-siblings or step-siblings. Some of these siblings may live with the child's family and others may not; thus it is not immediately apparent how many dependents some families actually have, but, in any case, overcrowded living conditions at home may not be amenable to a child-friendly environment.

G.K. Lieten and T. Strehl, *Child Street Life*, SpringerBriefs in Well-Being and Quality of Life Research 15, DOI 10.1007/978-3-319-11722-5_3

A social worker in Lima explained how such cramped and impoverished living conditions at home can result in a growing population of children living on the street:

> Have you seen the places they come from? For some children, there's hardly any difference between living on the street and sleeping at home on a cold floor with eight family members, without electricity or water. Especially if the child encounters family problems at home, the choice not to return home after a long day of street work is quickly made.

Some of the advantages of the street, that make children decide not to go home, are freedom, independence, close friendships, earning money and having control of their money and expenses. These characteristics of the street contrast with poverty, punishment, violence and lack of affection which the child may encounter at home. The *callejización* (street migration) consists of different stages of decision-making in which the child becomes more and more alienated from home and in which the family contacts diminish.

Although street living children commonly are characterised by the lack of regular family contact, many of them sporadically meet with parents or relatives. Most children in this research claimed to go home every now and then, generally every 2 or 3 months. Especially around Christmas many children expressed the desire to be with their family. At this time of the year they were more motivated to save money, look tidy and bring home savings and presents for relatives. Even though friends replace family on the streets, the children still continue to choose family over friends when asked who is more important (see also Tejada Ripalda 2005: 87). However, many children are too embarrassed or stressed to visit home. They are often afraid that family members won't accept them or disapprove of them and that they will be punished for having been away for so long.

Whenever street children do return home, they only stay a couple of days on average, before returning to the streets again. In most cases they immediately encounter the same problems that made them run away in the first place, and often they have become so adapted to street life that they can't feel comfortable with living between four walls anymore. Many children, however, expressed the desire to '1 day again be united with family members'. They apparently are in a continuous state of ambivalence.

Some children are actually still much attached to their family, as was the case of Juana (13). Although she can't live at home, because her step-father doesn't accept her, she tries to visit her mother every day and regularly yields some of her money to her mother for the care of her new-born half-sister. Also Arturo (15) visits his family regularly and feels responsible for the care of his alcoholic mother: 'I often walk her home after she has been in a *chicheria* (local corn beer pub), because otherwise she starts fighting with people on the street. I never sleep at home however; I don't like it there and the place is too small.' Jaime (13) returns home every now and then 'to have a good sleep, and cook a meal', but only when he knows that his mother is not at home.

Sometimes children even return home for a couple of weeks or months and temporarily re-establish their relationship with family members. This is often the case when children have severe problems with their health or are prosecuted by police. Fabian (13), for example, returned home for a couple of weeks when the police were threatening him with a forced stay in the juvenile detention centre. Diego (15), who lost family contact when he was 8 years old, re-established contact with his mother after he had broken his hand. Returning home was the only option, he argued, because with one hand he could not earn a living. As soon as he was better he left for the streets again.

In general, the mother is the family member most idealised and admired by street children. Even when children admitted to their mothers' violent behaviour, many spoke about her as the most valued person in their live. For example, Felix (13), who lived a short while in a rehabilitation centre for drug addicted street children in Lima: 'I love my mother a lot. I really hope she will come to visit me at Christmas. She is a really good and nice person.' Later I heard from educators that Felix was a severely traumatised child, because his mother used to tie him up on the bed for several days as a way of punishment. Also Naomi (12) idealised her mother: 'She is really cool. She looks beautiful and I feel sad that I have let her down by running away from home. Why did I run away? Well, she had a alcohol problem and every time she came home drunk she used to hit me. Our past was very difficult, but someday we will be united'. The eternal state of ambivalance—the need for emotional attachment with an idealized elder and the loathsome reality—may have dramatic consequences for the psychological balance of the street child.

3.2 Push Factors: Chucked-out or Run-away Children

This paragraph will focus mainly on the group of street-living children. In order to understand why children leave their homes and live on the street, we have to look at the different family situations they come from. Normally it is a combination of various push and pull factors that cause children to live on the streets.

The push-factors include, among others, domestic violence, parental alcoholism, low family income or unstable family income (children are sent to work to supplement the family's income), neglect and abuse, a poorly functioning school system, high tuition fees, poorly educated parents and the loss of parents: 'Running away from home is an act of resistance and an expression of absolute frustration with life circumstances. It is the strongest possible response to poverty and abuse that children in circumstances of deprivation and vulnerability can exercise' (Schimmel 2006: 212; see also Volpi 2002; Dybicz 2005). The pull-factors are aspects of street life that children experience as positive and as a way to escape the negative factors at home. Pull-factors, among others, include freedom, (economic) independence, friendship and love among (street) peers, opportunities to earn an income, drugs and the attraction of (social) entertainment in the city (e.g. internet cafés and game rooms).

Our quantitative survey confirms that that the majority of street-living children in Lima left their homes because of family problems (67 %). In Cusco, however, the main reason for not living with the family was the sheer fact that 41 % of the street-living children have no family in Cusco. What these children have in common, though, is that many come from economically poor families, living on the outskirts of the city in neighbourhoods popular among the migrants, or in the rural areas (particularly in Cusco).

Many families are dysfunctional. An extreme example of abysmal conditions of violence and criminality as the norm is the case of Livia's (12). Her father is one of the gang leaders in Campoy, a neighbourhood of El Augustino in Lima. He is known as the 'face cutter'. According to Livia, he knows how to cut faces, how to fight and how to drink, and most people are afraid of him. Livia too was afraid of him and joined a gang when she was 10 years old:

> My father was always walking with my auntie. She too drinks a lot and she slept with all the guys of the neighbourhood. Me too, I was always walking on the streets with the boys of the gang. They were the ones giving me alcohol and *terokal*. My father didn't want me to be with the gang and every time he saw me walking with them he beat me up. He said he wanted to cut my face too. That's why I didn't want to go home anymore. My father is a *piraña* (a bad guy), he gave me bad advice, so I walked away from home. I went to discothèques, casinos and hung around on the street.

An analysis of the children's personal histories and discussions with some of their parents and other family members,[1] showed how the reasons for the children ending up in the streets are diverse and that, possibly not surprisingly, explanations differed. The stories of the child and the parent often contradicted each other. Whereas in many cases violence and abusive family relations seemed to be at the centre of the children's testimonies, the parents' testimonies underlined the situation of poverty in which they lived and their children's bad and uncontrollable behaviour as the main factor.

A distinction can be made between the children that have been abandoned by their parents, the so-called thrown-away children, and the children that broke away from their families themselves, the so-called run-away children. Our observations found that far more children belonged to the latter category. Reasons for parents (or other family members) to abandon their children include, often in combination, poverty and a lack of economic resources, single-parented households or the entry of a step-parent and parental alcoholism and drug abuse.

An example is Diego (15), a middle child in a big and poor family, who has lived on the streets since he was 8 years old. One decade ago, his family moved to the outskirts of Cusco in search for work. His parents separated and his mother, with eight children to take care, every day travelled to the streets in the city centre

[1] Often it seemed to be difficult or impossible to meet their parents, because the parents had died, the children had no idea where their parents were, or the children didn't want us to meet their parents because of traumatic experiences in the past, shame, indifference or anxiety. In some cases we talked with other family members, like older brothers/sisters or aunties.

to sell food on the sidewalks, from early in the morning till late in the night. When she came home she used to bring her lovers. According to Diego he started to leave for the streets because he didn't feel any love at home and felt bored:

> My mother didn't care, I think she even hated me. She always brought home her boyfriends from the market, these dirty pigs! Yes, I saw it sometimes; they were having fun while we were trying to sleep. Our house was so small, just one room. I started to spend my days on the street, I hated it at home. There was no love. On the street I felt free, different from home.

Although still living at home, Diego felt attracted to street life because he saw in it an escape from the problems at home. He started to steal things from the house, which he then sold on the black market 'El Baratillo'. On the street, he got to know other street boys, who taught him to sniff glue. This exacerbated the strained relationship at home: 'My mother became really fed up with me; she said I was a criminal and that I better stay on the street. So she evicted me. I am the black sheep, that's what they say. For me my family doesn't exist; I don't have family.' When I visited his mother, a Quechua woman in poor health, she told me her version. She explained that she could not take care of him because of his 'lazy character':

> My son is a loafer, a liar. He never wanted to work or help us in the house. He was just passing his days on the street, doing really nothing, while we were starving. We are a big family and all of us are working to make a living, but he is the only one from our family that's like that. I am a single mother, how can I feed all my children? They have to help me, but Diego never wanted to.

The mutual dislikes between mother and son developed within a context of poverty, cramped housing and neglect of family life, possibly exacerbated by the mother's longing for adult intimacy and affection. Diego developed an unacceptable lifestyle that made the mother throw him out of the house. Problems at home pushed the boy into drug use as a way to escape these problems. It became a pull-factor. Within a context of poverty and material deprivation, the mother blamed her son, at that time only 8 years old, of her disability as a single-mother to take care of all her children.

The argument by some of the child-rights-based scholars that the street child should not be regarded as a victim but rather as an agent of change, as an active citizen, negates the basically unwarranted context in which these children are growing up and which pushes them onto the streets. Diego, for sure, exhibited agency; he decided what was best for him at that time. So were many other children whom we met and who often came from poor or abandoned single-parent families, mostly female-headed, in which the parent failed to take proper care of the child, either because of poverty or emotional and psychological instability.

Often also, the child was abandoned after the establishment of a new family unit, in which the step-parent refused to care for a child from another father or mother. One illustration is the case of Juana (13) who has been living on the streets of Cusco for the last 2 years. Her parents also grew up in the streets and had met each other in the same drop-in shelter as where Juana spends her nights.

She told us that after the loss of her father, who died of a drug-overdose, her alcoholic mother, married another man:

> I didn't get along with my step-father. He used to hit me with an iron pole on my head. He was like my father; he liked to drink. My step-father doesn't want me or my younger brothers to live at home. My mother is pregnant now; I think she has no choice. That's why my brothers live in a children's home and I live on the street. My mother loves that drunken guy more than she loves me. It makes me sad sometimes.

Something similar happened to Sharon (16). When she was 8 years old, her father landed in jail after killing the husband of his ex-wife. Her mother remarried, but the new husband wasn't interested in taking care of the children: 'He said that he didn't want to look after the children of another man, that we were not his problem'. Finally, Sharon's mother rented a small room in the centre of Cusco for her daughters to live in and disappeared with her new husband. The girls couldn't manage to pay the rent though, and ended up living on the streets. Also Jeremy (14) was pushed out. At the age of 4, he was abandoned by his (extremely) young mother when his father died. He was taken to his grandmother's house. The mother disappeared and when his grandmother died when Jeremy was 8 years old, he had no other place to go but the street. He told us: 'I hate my mother and I bear her a grudge, because she never wanted to know me'.

In some cases the single parent was forced to abandon his/her child after obtaining a far-away job or a job in which she/he had to travel a lot. This happened to Paul (11), whose mother died and whose father was a truck driver. He left his son with an aunt in Cusco, but Paul ran away because his aunty always punished him, wrongly he claims, for thefts. Situations similar to Paul's are not uncommon: children living with other relatives than their parents, or children living with the new family of their father or mother, are often given a subordinate place in the family and they often seem to bear the brunt when things are amiss or broken. They experience more exploitation, abuse and maltreatment compared to the other children. These children actually are both 'chucked-out disposed children' and 'run-away children': chucking-out relates to poverty and injustice, running-away relates to agency.

It is much more common for a child to run away from home, than for the parents (relatives) to kick out a child. The main reasons for running away, which the children mentioned, were economic exploitation, sexual or psychological abuse, parental alcoholism, and neglect or mistreatment by relatives. Instead of finding security, love and encouragement, the home actually may have turned into a place of discomfort and estrangement, or even fear. Working in the street is often a facilitator which helps the child in taking a decision not to return home anymore.

Although predictors for (working and) living on the streets are diverse (recent migration and dysfunctional family units among them), there is a relation between poor families sending their children to the streets as breadwinners and the permanent transfer of the child from home to the street. As they start spending a lot of time on the streets, children also start to compare advantages of street life with disadvantages of their home situation, with the option of finally replacing home life with street life (Tejada Ripalda 2005: 51–64). Many street-living children's testimonies show that the experience, which children had with street work at a young age, was instrumental for them starting to live on the street.

By spending a substantial time period on the street, children can become used to the 'freedom' and independence that street life offers, as was often mentioned: 'being able to keep the money', 'having no rules', 'playing', 'not having to travel long distances' and 'being able to steal and buy nice clothes'. Some children explained that they be friended children living on the streets, while working there, and that these street children taught them to use inhalants, mostly *terokal* (glue), and to play videogames. These working children then became addicted to these vices and no longer wanted to return home. The disinclination to return to the family fold would be exacerbated if the child knows that they would have to face their angry and dissatisfied parents.

Children hanging around in the streets are prone to 'the risk of children getting on the wrong track' and 'cross over onto the criminal path' (Ensing 2008). The archives of the street-child shelter *Generacion* in Lima, confirm that the majority of the street-living children started their permanent street life as ambulatory vendors, on an average starting at the age 8 (quoted in Tejada Ripalda 2005: 55). The testimonies of the children in our research are illustrative. This happened for example to Jaimer (14, Lima), who explained how street-work resulted in street-life for him:

> My street life actually started after my mother died. Before my mother died, she always took good care. When I was alone with my father it all changed. He was never at home. My older sister said 'Jaimer, you better work because otherwise we'll have nothing to eat.' That's when I went to the street to sell sweets; I was only 11 years old. On the Avenida Iquitos I met a group of street boys and I really liked how they dressed. I felt like a loser, wearing my crappy clothes. I started to befriend them and wanted to be like them. That's when I tried *terokal* (glue). It made me forget my problems at home. After a while I decided to stay with them on the street and I started to sleep on the porch of a church. Drugs have brought me many bad things, they made me leave home. Now it's too late to go back.

Jaimer has found a new lifestyle, and actually is a good specimen of an ingenious and resilient child, but he actually loathes it and still longs for a normal childhood. He has reflected on the fragility of life under conditions of structural poverty and family distress, and disapproves of the fact that many parents in Lima send their children to work: 'They should work themselves and the children should stay at home to study. But here in Lima many parents are bad and want their children to earn the money. They don't see the consequences.'

Jaimer's journey into the street trade, unlike that of most young children working on the streets, was not supervised by adults. Older family members usually keep an eye on the younger ones, preventing them from getting involved with drug-use or criminal street children. However, also in this case the process of street migration can take place if the child feels his or her work is not appreciated by the parents or when the child encounters problems at home. An example is Sandra (15), who had been selling goods on the Plaza de Armas in Cusco with her mother ever since she was 5 years old. When she turned 13, after encountering and befriending other children who had made the street into their home and whose living conditions were not unnecessarily more destitute than hers, she started to withdraw from her mother:

> At home we suffered a lot and I had to give all the money to my mum. I wanted to keep my own money and I was always afraid that my mother would hit. But the street has really messed me up, because I didn't want to go home anymore after work. Sometimes I stayed 3 or 4 days on the street, waking up on the Plaza. I befriended many *pirañas* (street kids) on the Plaza and I wanted to stay with them. I started to like stealing and buying myself new clothes. That's why I hardly returned home anymore.

Another common situation is that parents living in the impoverished countryside send their children to live with other people (mostly relatives) in bigger cities, hoping that the child will have better prospects. This process explains why a large percentage of street-living children (Lima 25 %, Cusco 41 %) claimed not to have a family to live with. Expectations, both of parents and children, of 'the good life in the city', with better working and educational opportunities, frequently pull rural children to Lima's and Cusco's streets. When life in the city turns out to be much more difficult than expected, or when the relatives turn out to be less than benign, street life beckons. We met children as young as 5 or 6, mostly accompanied by older siblings, walking the streets of Lima and Cusco selling *caramelos* (sweets) and *tostaditas* (dried seeds) to be able to pay for a room at a cheap hostel for the night. The family members they had come to live with either hadn't accepted them or had exploited or mistreated them, resulting in the children living on the streets. Although their migration to the city did not turn out as they expected, i.e. they were not able to go to school or to save money, they did not return home because of shame, unattractive living conditions in their home villages, and the habituation to city and street life.

3.3 Pull Factors

City life, with the illusion of freedom and relief from problems at home, has attracted many enterprising young kids. Many children explained how they had the idea before coming to Cusco that it would be easy to make money, because '*los pavos*[2] spend their money easily'. By migrating to Cusco the children, like many adults, had hoped to get a slice of the tourist pie by working informal jobs on the street. Filipo (11), for example, had arrived in Cusco from the countryside, with his cousin, 2 months previously:

> I was so bored at home; I was always alone with my younger brothers and sisters. My mother wanted me to wash their clothes and cook our food. If I was not helping in the house, I had to look after our cattle, waking up at 3 o'clock. Ai! My mother never cared about how I felt and she liked to command. When my cousin Braulio told me he was going to earn a lot of money in Cusco, I didn't hesitate to accompany him. Now I keep my own money and buy new shoes. My parents? They don't know.

---

[2] Literally this means 'turkeys', but in street dialect the term is used for 'tourists'.

Deprived living conditions often lead to strained relationships in the home, causing stress to parents and children alike. The overbearing responsibilities in the household and the lack of basic needs, like food, love, attention and diversion resulted in the children leaving for the streets in search of independence, material satisfaction and social bonding with peers. The phenomenon of the street child thus actually is very much a class issue, namely the inhuman living conditions and the bleak prospects for any improvement which so many families are coping with. This line of analysis is usually overlooked by the many authors who have tended to focus on interactional features, particularly at the ingenious ways in which children survive in the cities' streets, if they do.

Material poverty, and the need for the child to work, is not the only feature associated with poverty. In some cases not material poverty, but the lack of love, affection and security, were felt as the decisive problems at home. Maltreatment and alcoholism were often mentioned. Many of these children, who have faced violence at home, feel safer on the streets. Juan (17) left home when he was only 5 years old for such reasons, i.e. maltreatment, parental alcoholism and neglect:

> I left home because my parents were alcoholics. My father beat me when he was drunk. One day my mother tried to poison me and I had to go to the hospital. She didn't want to have us; many of my brothers died. From 9 brothers, only 4 are still alive. Nobody came to the hospital to visit me, so when I was healthy, they (the hospital staff) just kicked me out on the streets. There I got to know drugs.

Afterwards, Juan had been captured by the police and was placed in a children's home, but he ran away. He explained that if you are already used to the freedom of the street ('having no roof, feeling the sun on your face and walking around wherever you want and whenever you want'), it is hard to become used to life 'in a place with walls'. If a child chooses to leave street life, as most street children have at some/several points in their life, relatively few children actually manage to stay in the children's homes for very long. They find it exceedingly difficult to live according to all the rules and regulations. Sometimes street child organisations overlook the fact that street children are very much imbedded socially, culturally and economically in street life and that ties with the street cannot be broken from one day to the next. The more drug-addicted and adapted a child is to street life, the harder it is to offer adequate help and get the child of the streets.

Domestic violence and the attraction of street life as a better alternative to it, was explicitly mentioned by Jaime (13). His father often turned violent and he loathed living conditions at home ('we have no TV, not even light, and there's nothing to do'). Like many other street children, Jaime already befriended other street children before he left his house. After living for 1 year on the street, and after his father had died, he went back to his mother's house for a couple of months, but he couldn't get used to it: 'My mother was always pressuring me to help her with her work in the canteen, waking up at 4 'o clock, no, no, I said, I prefer to live on the street then.' When we visited his mother's small loam-stone house, the neighbour explained how she wasn't surprised that Jaime was on the streets, because 'that woman is never at home, always working'. The absence of parents at home, mostly due to work, often results in the children doing whatever they want; for example, hanging out in the streets or in internet cafés with friends instead of going to school. Little by little the children are introduced to street life, come into contact with children that use drugs and become accustomed to the freedom of the streets.

In Lima, some of the interviewed children mentioned violence and gang culture in their neighbourhoods as one of the pull-factors that landed them on the streets. Many poor neighbourhoods of Lima are ruled by violent gangs or *pandillas*. Many street children were in contact with these gangs and several children had their first contact with drugs through gang members in their neighbourhood. The gang members were seen as role models. Problems at home pushed children into the street gangs in the neighbourhood, which were often the start of the transition to street life. The gangs introduced the children to street life, drugs, crime and sometimes even prostitution.

Also John (17), who already has a 4 year old child, started street life in a street gang. He hails from a violent neighbourhood in Callao, Lima, but now lives on the streets of the city centre, playing music in buses:

I was *pandillero* (gang member) since I was 11 years old. My father was a drunkard and abused me a lot. My mother had left the place. That's why I joined the gang. My uncle was already a member of the gang. When I was 12, I learned how to handle a revolver. When I was 14 years I entered Maranga (youth prison), because I had killed another *pandillero* with a bullet.

The last case illustrates a process from bad to worse. Transitions take place all the time: transition from acceptable to bad, from bad to worse and from worse to a death-trap. Transition is the key for understanding the street child phenomenon. Children who have a deplorable home condition and who, for various reasons, flock to the street, are in danger of moving from an acceptable life style to a full-fledged street life. The distinction between on-the-street and of-the-street is a valid one since it helps us to understand the various modes of street life, but also, importantly, the constant risk of a transition process. The street migration consists of different stages of decision-making in which the freedom of street life beckons and the child becomes more and more alienated from home. The discrete categories have been abandoned in recent research and researchers, writing from a child agency perspective, claim to have constructed more revealing typologies. Thomas de Benitez (2011: 8, writing for the Consortium for Street Children) concludes: 'Definitions reflect tensions between policy/intervention planning and social researchers' increasing focus on children's experiences'. The voices of the children represented here actually suggest that the 'of' and 'on' perspective is valid, and actually that intervention policies should very much take care of the constant risk of the 'children on the street' moving into the category of 'children of the street'.

References

Dybicz, P. (2005). Interventions for street children. An analysis of current best practices. *International Social Work, 48*(6), 763–771.

Ensing, A. (2008). *Child labour in the urban sectors of Peru*. Amsterdam: IREWO.

Schimmel, N. (2006). Freedom and autonomy of street children. *The International Journal of Children's Rights, 14*, 211–233.

Tejada Ripalda, L. (2005). *Los niños de la calle y su mundo*. Lima: Fondo Editorial de la Facultad de Ciencias Sociales, Universidad Nacional de San Marcos.

Thomas de Benitez, S. (2011). *State of the world's street children: Research*. London: Consortium of Street Children.

Volpi, E. (2002). *Street children. Promising practices and approaches*. Washington: The World Bank Working Papers (26388).

Chapter 4
Street Life

Street life hardly had any of the positive aspects which recently have been associated with 'agency'. Living in the streets means submitting to gang culture and gang violence. Once a street-working child starts living on the street permanently, hazards such as violence, harassment, sexual abuse, drug addiction and health problems abound. The needs that street-living children express are not so much related to material needs—their living conditions earlier were not necessarily better while living at home—but more to emotional needs. This of course applies much more to children living in the street (the thus-called children of the street) than to children working in the street.

Whereas in the last quarter of the twentieth century reporting on street children abounded in terms of pity, exploitation, misery and condemnation, recent anthropological studies tend to emphasize choice, agency, resilience and survival. Street life, according to some recent interpretations, has been misrepresented by media and human rights activists. Emphasis, according to that interpretation, has wrongly been on the vulnerabilities and on the street child as a victim. The life of these children is stated to have many positive aspects: they are developing their own 'identity' and actually suffer more from 'discrimination because they are labelled and targeted' (Ennew 1995: 402). In studies by Panter-Brick, it is argued that the of-the-street children often fared quite well in terms of nutritional status, health and clothing and that 'urban homelessness may represent an appropriate response to circumstances of poverty' (quote in Woan et al. 2013: 3; see also Panter-Brick 2002; Bourdillon et al. 2010: 135–139). The intensive study of numerous street children in different parts of two cities, both on-the street and off-the street children, will help to put the debate in perspective.

The overview (Table 4.1) indicates that many children do not encounter any problem. This may relate more to the children who spend only a few hours per day in the streets (8 % in Lima and 17 % in Cusco less than 3 h/day, and half of the children spend more than 3 h but less than 9 h). Harassment (physical and

G.K. Lieten and T. Strehl, *Child Street Life*, SpringerBriefs in Well-Being and Quality of Life Research 15, DOI 10.1007/978-3-319-11722-5_4

Table 4.1 Frequency of street-life-related problems of all street children

	Lima	Cusco	Percentage
None	146	102	23.7
Verbal violence	145	71	20.7
Physical violence	84	21	10.2
Sexual harassment	35	4	3.7
Discrimination	46	10	5.4
Robberies and criminals	59	5	6.1
Lack of money and job opportunity	127	45	16.5
Health problems	50	38	8.5
Traffic problems	25	4	2.8
Others	16	9	2.4
Total	733	309	100

Source Irewoc, Tablas Estadísticas—Niños y Niñas de la calle en Lima y Cusco (Table 23)

psychological) and discrimination and the lack of money were frequently mentioned in both cities; in Lima robberies and sexual harassment were an additional factor of insecurity.

4.1 Settling Down in the Street

Street children in Lima reside in different locations in different neighbourhoods, mostly around commercial areas and markets, and stay by and large with the same group of children, called *mancha* or *battería*. Within their own location they move around a lot, but generally without leaving the area. The specific location where a child resides becomes part of his/her identity and contact between children from different areas is rare.[1] As in Lima, street children in Cusco are highly mobile, both in their (labour) activities and in their locations, but their mobility does not stop at the ward borders or even city borders, as most children have travelled at some time in their life to other places in Peru, in search for work. Popular places among street children are commercial areas and entertainment centres outside the

[1] While in the eighties and nineties street children in Lima were mainly found in the city centre around the main squares and on the river banks of the river Rímac, in the last decade commercial areas in the outskirts of the city, the *conos*, also saw a growing street child population. In the city centre, while Plaza San Martin, Parque Universitario and the riverbanks of Rímac were popular places a couple of years ago, nowadays the children move to more obscure places like the prostitution zone of Avenida Grau and Iquitos, and passages around the big traffic street of Abancay. However, despite the heavy police oppression in the River Rímac area a small group of adolescents and youngsters still live here, among them are the most deteriorated and addicted street children with signs of dementia and schizophrenia.

historic centre, like in and around markets, shopping streets and areas with a high density of restaurants and bars catering for Peruvians. At night, they also sleep in the municipal's dormitory or rarely in internet cafés, dilapidated buildings, in the hills around Cusco, under bridges or on the pavements.

The children in their locality are acquainted with gang culture and gang members actually use street children for drug trafficking or assaults. Each child arriving on the street tries to become part of a particular *battería* (gang) as a means of survival. The process is a gradual one, involving various stages and the gradual replacement of home ties with street ties (Visano 1990; Rizzini and Butler 2003). Persy (14) from Lima explained how he was integrated into street life:

> At first it was difficult; I didn't know anything about the street. But after 2 or 3 days I got to know other street kids. Their attitudes were different from mine; they acted more like gangsters. Then I started to wash cars and even beg for money. Later on I learned how to play instruments and how to steal. I started to take drugs and drunk a lot. I learned how to speak *jerga* (slang). Once you know street slang, you only speak slang.

Becoming part of a street group is not easy though and a child first has to 'prove' that he/she really belongs to the street and to get acquainted with the 'subculture of the streets'. By watching and participating in street life, new children learn to cope with and adapt to their new environment, as Jeremy (14) explained:

> I joined the gang because I felt very lonely. I had nobody. There is one boss, *el jefe*, and he told me to first rob a purse from a girl, before I could enter the gang. I had to prove that I was not a wimp. Being with them I felt more secure than being alone. I was the youngest of the group and the others treated me with love; they gave me food and clothes. Whenever I was detained in the *comisaria* (police station), the older ones would come to get me out, saying they were my brothers and paying some hush money.

Within the group of street children a delicate social distinction is made based on the level to which the child has adapted to street life and street culture; this distinction defines his/her place in the street hierarchy. Not knowing how to steal or talking in street slang, can result in exclusion or, even worse, in bullying and (sexual) abuse. Being accepted on the street, and becoming affiliated with a certain street group, is about knowing the rules and habits that characterise street life. For example, Wilmer (13) lives on the streets of Cusco. When we first noticed him, he was shyly standing in front of a restaurant, playing uneasily with his *conchas* (shells that are used as a music instrument). His clothes were dirty and one sleeve of his sweater was torn. He looked like a 'real' street child to us, but the other street boys, when we asked them if Wilmer was also a street boy, started to laugh: 'This *zonzo* (idiot)? Do you really think he's from the street? He doesn't even dare to enter [the restaurant]. And look at his clothes, nobody will take him serious!' It was clear that our (stereotypical) idea of a street child didn't match theirs. It turned out that the boys were right in their assessment; Wilmer had only been living on the streets for two weeks. A couple of weeks later we saw a different kind of Wilmer. He was wearing a flashy red hat, new sneakers and he was accompanied by the same boys whom we had been walking with that first day. Proudly Wilmer showed us his catch of the day: 2 stolen car mirrors, worth 10 soles (2.60 euro) each. Being a good thief, using drugs and dressing well, are highly valued markers of street life. These characteristics are related; if you know how to get 'quick money' through stealing, you are able to buy (expensive) drugs and nice clothes (Rizzini and Butler 2003; Wolseth 2010).

4.2 Characteristics of Street-Living Children

Street life in Lima and Cusco is characterised by a high degree of drug consumption among street-living children. While most street-working children don't use any substances, in both cities around 62 % of the street-living children do use substances. The most common drugs are alcohol (58 %) and the glue *Terokal* (47 %). At all times of the day street-living children can be seen inhaling glue, although consumption is highest in the evenings and night time. *Terokal* is mainly inhaled from plastic bags and sometimes from plastic bottles. Other popular drugs are marihuana (20 %) and *pasta* (19 %), a cocaine-based paste which is especially harmful, physically and psychologically. Also Diazepam, a drug to treat insomnia or anxiety, is regularly used. The children in Lima are remarkably beyond shame. Contrary to children in Cusco, most street children in Lima continue inhaling *Terokal* in front of outsiders and social workers from NGOs.

In Lima, children sleep in porches, parks and dark alleys, and under bridges and viaducts at night, but many nowadays in winter sleep in unofficial illegal hostels, where a bed costs a few soles per night. In general, these hostels are dirty crammed places where children mingle with (street) adults, drug use is high, and sexual abuse is common. Compared to Lima, which has a more moderate climate, few children in Cusco regularly spend the whole night on the street. Most street-living children return to a municipal dormitory, cheap hostel, rented room, internet café or abandoned house at night.

In Cusco, we hardly met any girl living in the street. In comparison, there is a relatively high number of street-living girls visible on the streets in Lima, especially in street prostitution on the Avenida Grau and in La Parada, the area around Lima's biggest wholesale markets. The street-living children in this area are among the most deteriorated and forgotten group of children. Whereas street girls that don't work in prostitution generally wear dirty oversized clothes, girls that prostitute themselves are generally dressed in sexy and tight outfits, often have piercings and tattoos and wear a lot of make-up.

A relatively high number of the prostitutes are addicted teenage mothers. Although some adolescent mothers accommodate their children with adult family members, others keep their babies and small children with them. This way a second generation of street children is bred. Some mothers will continue their drug consumption during pregnancy or consume glue in presence of their babies, who already show signs of brain damage or malnourishment. Other mothers, on the contrary, stay clear of drugs once they know they are pregnant.

In contrast to street boys, there are few girls that really sleep on the street. Although during the day, they spend a lot of time on the street with other street children and street gangs, many of these girls sleep in hostels, at friend's houses or with family members. They also spend a lot of time with friends in discotheques and so called *antros* (obscure nightclubs). Street girls are vulnerable to sexual exploitation, maltreatment, sexual abuse and (gang) rapes (see also Mayuntupa 2006), and therefore search for protection among the street boys or adults, who in many cases demand sexual favours in exchange. Sex work is often promoted by street friends or relatives as an easy way to earn money. For instance, Naomi (12), who escaped from her alcoholic mother and has lived on the streets for the past two years, explained:

> My cousin, who is 16, was already working in prostitution and one day she asked me to join her. I was 11 then. She said it is very easy and that we can earn a lot. Well, in that time I was already using drugs, like *mixto* [smoking *pasta* with marihuana] and *bembos* [smoking cocaine with marihuana]. I wanted money to buy more drugs and I had to pay for my room. We charged 100 soles (26 euros) each time. I didn't like the job, but in 15 min I earned more than other friends did in a week!

4.3 Income Generation and Expenses

Other studies (see for example Wolch and Rowe 1993; Ruddick 1996; Wolseth 2010; Gigengack 2006) have argued that street children seem to be on a constant search for the best possible opportunities of income generation, emotional affection and access to resources. Most street-living children use the street for income generation, as they work independently on the squares, main roads, sidewalks and alleys of Lima and Cusco. Income generation activities, however, are limited. The children necessarily focus on activities with low remuneration, low social status and insecure income.

In the survey, the activities of the children at the time of the interview have been recorded (see Table 4.2). Some activities probably suffer from underrepresentation, either because it was not happening at that particular point of time or because the children felt inhibited to mention. Robbing, begging and prostitution are only occasionally mentioned as an activity which they were currently engaged in or which they usually did (*la actividad que más haces en la calle*). These activities are likely to occur more frequently among street-living children. The overall statistics only confirm that the children are dexterously active, particularly in selling goods and in providing some street services, such as *lustrabota* (shoe cleaners) and *cargador* (goods carriers).

Only a few of the street-living children perform wage labour. Others mentioned that at some stage in their life they had been employed, but they all seemed to agree that they were better off working independently on the streets. The informal and often socially undesirable work on the streets has the advantages of 'the freedom of being your own boss' and of 'defining your own work schedule', to be 'independent and free', to be 'earning my own money' and not to be exploited. Antonio, for instance, revealed that he likes polishing shoes 'because I can quit

Table 4.2 Current and usual activities of the street children

	Current activities			Usual activities as reported		
	Lima	Cusco	Percentage	Lima	Cusco	Percentage
Selling	351	154	43.1	474	184	47.1
Service	184	66	21.4	228	81	22.0
Strolling/playing	144	92	20.2	95	62	11.2
Leisure, resting	30		2.6			
Begging	23	3	2.2	55		3.9
Accompanying a family member	20		1.7	28		2.0
Juggling/acrobatics	14	5	1.6	26	11	2.6
Playing music/performing for tourists	14	9	2.0	34	27	4.3
Drugs use	14		1.2			
Prostitution				9	0	0.6
Other activity	34	14	4.1	61	32	6.6
Total	828	343	100	1,010	397	100

Source Irewoc, Tablas Estadísticas—Niños y Niñas de la calle en Lima y Cusco (Tables 1 and 2)

work whenever I want to play soccer with the other street workers, any day of the week'. As a wage labourer, he would have to forego that option.

Some children explained how they had left their former jobs because they were abused by their employers, being underpaid and exploited, but quite often also it appeared that they had lost their jobs because they failed to show up and couldn't comply with the rules. Most of the reasons for these children not wanting or not being able to be employed are related to characteristics typical to street children, i.e. having a lack of structure in their life, little persistence in difficult situations and non-compliance with rules.

Street-living children have different strategies for making a living, ranging from labour activities (such as shining shoes, carrying goods, pulling carts and collecting garbage) to illicit activities, such as stealing and drug trafficking, and to performances with a variety of musical instruments. Other economic activities include acrobatic performances and windscreen cleaning at traffic junctions, washing cars, guarding cars, cleaning tombstones at the cemetery and begging, including requesting food at restaurants.

Sex work is another activity street children can engage in, particularly in Lima. This activity takes on different forms, such as sex-for-commodity relationships with tourists (known as *bricherismo*), sex-for-money with Peruvians and tourists in hidden alleyways, closed markets or hotel rooms and street girls (and boys) offering sex to street boys in exchange for food, small gifts and drugs. All this amounts to 'survival sex' (Woan et al. 2013: 4). The vulnerability of street children makes them prone to different kinds of (sexual) exploitation and abuse. For both boys and girls, it is common to maintain (sexual) relationships with adults in exchange for care, protection and sometimes commodities (on Lima, see also

Gigengack 1998; Alarcón 1994). In Lima centre, for example, several street children claimed to be 'friends' with an adult who gives them food, a place to sleep and care in exchange for sexual favours. The ambivalent relation between the boys and the adult is shown in Jaimer's (14) description: 'He always helps me. He protects me, so other boys will not hit me. He gives me food whenever I am hungry. When I am tired he lets me sleep in his bed. Sometimes he wants me to be his girlfriend. That's okay, because he is my only friend.'

In most cases street children combine different strategies or switch regularly between legal and illegal income generating activities. William, a 13-year-old postcard vendor, explained how he combines legal and illegal activities for his income generation: 'If I don't sell enough postcards to buy myself a meal, I'll try to earn some money in a different way; sometimes pick-pocketing a tourist while I pretend to chat with him.' Jeremy (14) explained how his shift from legal to illegal activities was related to drug addiction:

> My street life started after my grandmother died. I saw another kid singing in restaurants, so I imitated him to earn some money. After one month I got to know a place where street children sleep. I befriended them and they brought me in contact with *Terokal*. Then I started to drink. That's when I started to steal cell phones, to be able to buy my drugs.

Most jobs performed by street children are low in the social hierarchy of street work: shoe shiners, postcard sellers, singing, car washing or guarding cars (Steel 2008: 86). Jeremy (14) explained: 'I felt ashamed when I was singing in a *cevichería* (fish restaurant), people look at you as if you're a *ratero* (thief). You can even hear them think "bastard" and they say "fuck off" if you pass by.' Jaime (15) also was deeply aware of the discrimination and contempt: 'They think that you are really a loser in life; that you're not educated and good for nothing'. The street children indeed exhibit behaviour that doesn't agree with the general image of the 'good child' in society and they are very much aware of their social exclusion and stigma of being, among others, 'drug addicts', 'thieves', 'dirty', 'dangerous' and 'spoilt'. The stigma is reflected in the nicknames they are given in Peruvian society: *ratones* (rats), *pirañas* (piranha), *terokalero* and *fumones* (smokers of drugs). Many street children complained about being given these names, like Gustavo (15): 'Most of the time people don't want to help me. If I ask them for food they won't give it to me. They say 'go to work *piraña, fumon*!' That's not fair; they just call us these names because we live on the street. But I am also a human being, just like them'. Antonio (16) expressed the same problems: 'My friends taught me how to sing, but I always felt ashamed to ask people for money after the song. People say many bad words to you; they say that you're a loafer and a beggar. Therefore singing makes me feel sad.'

Contrary to the stereotypical image of street-living children, many of them have money to spend. The average income of a street-living child in our sample lies between 10 soles (2.60 euro) and 50 soles (13 euro) a day. They keep all their money themselves, which makes them financially better-off than their street-working peers who have to hand over most of their money to their relatives. Some studies have even suggested that street-working children have lower nutritional status than the street-living (on-the-street) children (especially the study by Panter-Brick 2002; see also Woan et al. 2013: 3). They often buy food, candies and soft drinks and they regularly buy new fashionable clothes. The reverse side of the coin is that on other days, they just eat the leftovers in restaurants or sleep on the street. The insecure life situation and economic vulnerability of street children is clearly summarized in Carlos's (16) statement: 'Sometimes it happens that I don't earn in the morning, I don't earn in the afternoon and I don't earn at night, well, then I just endure till the next day'.

Street children are very inventive in finding ways to earn money. In their work they use their talents in the best possible ways, i.e. their talent in convincing people, in looking needy, in making music or in acrobatics. They know the importance of playing on the emotions of possible clients. They are conscious that people give money more easily when they play the role of 'hungry street child'. Adolescent street kids making music in restaurants often prefer to play with a younger (and cute looking) street child. Charly (9), for example, was a popular companion for older boys to work with. They would address the audience before starting a song with the following introduction:

> Good afternoon, dear audience. The ones talking to you are some guys, trying to make a living with music. I want you to meet my little brother, he's just 9 years old and orphan already. Look at him, he's starving of hunger. Our life is miserable, our uncles are drunkards. By playing music we try to maintain ourselves and little brothers. Instead of stealing we make a living in a humble way. My brother will pass by for contributions, knocking the doors of your hearts. Thanks in advance!

In reality they were neither brothers, nor orphans, nor hungry at that moment. Afterwards they share the money and either spend it on drugs or on recreational activities.

Other successful strategies, to name just a few, are: 'being nice to tourists by making jokes and talking English', 'insisting when clients deny', 'being cute' and 'wearing clean clothes'. Knowing how to approach and befriend tourists is another survival strategy. Carlos, a 16 year old shoe shiner, described his strategy of getting tourists to pay high prices for his services: 'I always let the tourist decide what to pay; I'll say "*a su voluntad*" (at your convenience), and sometimes they give 30 or 40 soles (8–10 euro)!' The tourists' lack of knowledge about local prices means they often donate/tip more than expected.

Another popular way of income generation for street-living children is petty thievery. Besides pick-pocketing (purses, watches and cell-phones) and bag snatching, especially the theft of exterior car mirrors is popular. Some boys are more successful in stealing than others, which in turn affects their social status within the street group. Once a child is used to earning 'easy money' and buying whatever he/she wants, it is hard to kick the habit of stealing. The thrill of stealing also seems to be addictive; some children described stealing as just another vice like gaming and drugs.

Within street culture, a specialised vocabulary has developed; they use the words *laburar* ('to work') and *cobrar* ('to charge someone') to refer to stealing. The latter word suggests that street children feel that they have the right to the belongings of someone else. Notions of inequality in society and the lack of other options for income generation are at the core of their justification of thieving activities. Julio commented: 'I just steal from rich people. They have everything and we have nothing. You can recognise a rich person by the way he walks and dresses; they move around in cars and eat in restaurants'. The discursive legitimization notwithstanding, the *laburar* and *cobrar* are also performed on other street children. It is common in street culture that the older boys steal money and clothes from the younger ones. Either they openly command the youngsters to give them their money, or things are stolen in a more secret manner. Many street children said not to have any savings, because they prefer to spend their earned money immediately on food, drugs, new (fashion) clothes or internet and videogames, rather than having it stolen by other street children.

Delinquency is high, and street children in common sense understanding are often branded as drug-consuming thieves. Paradoxically, many children feel they have no other option than to steal, because outsiders treat them like delinquents when they try to earn money honestly (see also Gigengack 1998: 415). They are referred to as *ratones* and *pirañas* and some children explained that 'people oblige you to steal'. It is their own fault, they say: because they were not willing to help street children, they are the target of *cobrar*. It is a vivid example of blaming the victim. In any case, it helps to legitimize what they are doing, but it indeed exposes a real dilemma, which was clearly formulated by Ricardo (12) in the following words: 'When I am stealing, people tell me to go and work. When I am working, selling candies, the police confiscate my merchandise. How am I going to work if the police won't let me? My only option is to *laburar*, so I can afford a bed for the night'. Such explanations tend to endorse the stereotype of street children as young criminals, but we also met a number of children who said that they still prefer low status jobs to immoral and illegal activities. Hector (16) commented: 'If you steal, you harm other people. You take their money and valuables in a second, while they have been working a long time to achieve it. Before, I stole purses, cell-phones and mp3s with my friends. Now I have a more humble job. I make music and feel better about myself'.

4.4 Social Relations on the Street

Having friends and being part of a group is important for reasons of affection, understanding and safety. It provides a feeling of social belonging that was generally absent in their former family relationships. The street group is often spoken of as a kind of family. Children refer to their friends as 'brothers and sisters' or 'uncles' and solidarity between them is high. As Juan (17) explained: 'We all eat with the same spoon and sleep side by side. No matter if someone has tuberculosis or even AIDS, we are not averse to this person'. Ramon (14) explained the importance of his best friend: 'He is like my brother; we respect each other a lot. He never hits me. Whenever he has money he gives it to me, to buy new shoes. He gives me good advice and helps me if policemen are chasing me'. Friends on the street thus function as a substitute family. They pay attention and provide the affection, which the children didn't get from their own families at home. Jherson (17) commented about his friend:

> I have known Antonio since we worked together in the bakery. We are fighting a lot, but at the end we always give each other a hand. We have to do that, because we live together day and night. We are each other's only help, because our parents have forgotten about us. We help each other, because we are alone, without family. We live the same disastrous life.

But friendships on the street can be threatening also, as Jherson suggested. Arguments and fights, mostly related to girlfriends, money or drugs, are common. Being part of a street group thus seems a necessity, but children can clearly identify its negative sides. They mentioned that their friends sometimes maltreat them, steal their money or have a bad influence on them. Peer pressure is high and is an important aspect that makes it difficult for children to leave street life. Children who have the desire to enter a children's home are sometimes stopped by their friends. It seems to be almost impossible for a child to maintain his/her new lifestyle, without drugs and with an education, while still roaming around with the same street friends. Children often blame their friends for their bad habits. Diego (15): 'Sometimes I don't like my friends; they push me into bad things. They say "come for a *flight* [trip]", and if I don't join them they will bully me, so I have to join them'. Hector (15) added: 'I also have many bad friends, they steal and use drugs. If I tell them "look, I have changed", they make fun of me and say "look at this saint"'.

Sports and play occupy an important place in daily life. The streets are not only an environment to work in, but are also seen as a venue for entertainment and fun. Street children are often seen playing cards on the sidewalks, running after each other on the squares, playing soccer games in parks and football pitches or simply just 'hanging out' ('*hacer hora*', literally: 'waiting for the right time'). This hanging around and playing on the streets are important factors to the sensation of freedom that street children experience. In the summer time Lima's beaches are also an important space for leisure. The green hills that surround Cusco are also attractive, and offer limitless opportunities for fun. Street children also spend a considerable amount of time in dance halls, cinemas, swimming pools and leisure parks. And they spend several hours per day in cyber cafes, video arcades and pinball rooms. The popularity of internet among street children is a new phenomenon. Especially social network sites, chat programmes, music videos on YouTube, games and pornographic pictures and movies are popular.

4.5 Consequences of Living on the Street

Once a street-working child starts living on the street permanently, hazards such as violence, sexual abuse, drug addiction and health problems abound. The needs that street-living children express are not so much related to material needs—their living conditions earlier were not necessarily better—but more to emotional needs.

Table 4.3 Major problem associated with street life (street-living and street-working children)

	Lima (Nr)	Cusco (Nr)	Combined (%)
None	115	40	10.1
Violence, thefts	211	142	22.9
Poverty	148	102	16.2
Family problems	196	80	17.9
Compulsion to work	93	20	7.3
Drugs	83	22	6.8
Discrimination and insults	55	58	7.3
Exclusion from education	46	13	3.8
Street life in itself	8	4	0.9
Others	60	14	4.8
No response	24	7	2.0
	1,039	502	100

Source Irewoc, Tablas Estadísticas—Niños y Niñas de la calle en Lima y Cusco (Table 34); in some cases, more than one answer has been recorded

They miss belonging to a family, of having someone that really cares for them. They barely mentioned not having a house as their main problem, but emphasised drug-addiction, lack of education, a lack of positive prospects, discrimination by the public, violence and maltreatment by the police, as their main problem (see Table 4.3). Loneliness also was often mentioned, despite the positive reference to the street friends as a family of safety and belonging. The children may exhibit 'agency' and may have constructed a type a comradeship with their peers, but the need for a proper family- and home-environment, often breaks through, like in the words of Josue (12), when he talked about his favourite animal: 'My favourite animal is a parrot. He gives you company whenever you feel lonely. In the street you always feel lonely, yes, I am really lonely.' Deteriorating family relations is a recurrent problem which street-living children referred to as a consequence of street life. When talking about family, street children regularly switched between blaming weak family relationships for their need to live on the streets, to blaming their street life for the poor relationships with their families. Children, for example Freddy (14), often mentioned having been hurt by their parents and that they absolutely missed the love and attention of a family:

> To feel the love of your family is something beautiful. A mother who shows you her love and that you can ask your father interesting questions. But with my parents I never felt love. They fight a lot and my mother hits her sons. It has always been like that; a lack of understanding.

Lisandro (15) despises his parents for never giving him attention:

> My parents are like strangers, because they didn't show me their love when I needed it most. Living on the street when you are a boy of 7 or 8 years old is not easy. Those days I needed their warmth, but now it's too late.

The children recounted the horrible things their parents had done to them, leading to their escape, but they also realized the difficulty of restoring family relationships, feeling ashamed of their lifestyle and drug abuse.

One of the factors that exacerbate the children's exclusion from society is their substance use and abuse. Health workers and street educators list respiratory problems, such as bronchitis and tuberculosis, skin infections, malnutrition, diarrhoea, injuries, bad teeth and psychological defects as the most frequent health problems. Continuous substance abuse also tends to exacerbate psychological problems such as schizophrenia, anxiety, depression and even psychosis. Drugs are unanimously being mentioned by street-living children in Lima and Cusco as a problem related to street life. Some children literally described themselves as 'drug addicted losers'. In a group discussion in Lima, the boys pointed out that especially *terokal* and *pasta*, 'destroys your lungs', 'makes you crazy', 'makes you forget all what's important', 'makes you do bad things' and 'is a vice you can't get rid of'. Besides the negative effects which drugs are known to have on someone's health, the children also estimated that drugs were the core cause of bad habits like stealing, fighting, prostituting and being unfriendly to other people. Gustavo (15), for example, said: 'Since I got addicted I started to steal. Drugs brought me all bad things, because I do everything to get money for my trip. Once I almost killed someone with a knife, just to get his coins. I had no money for a can of *terokal* and I totally freaked out. They are evil. It's a vice, but I can't help it'.

When asked what children do if they face problems, the most common answer was 'just endure'. The vulnerability of street children makes them prone to different kinds of violence and (sexual) exploitation and abuse. Although all street children mentioned to be subject to violence, it is the emotionally and physically weaker who bear the brunt. Jaimer (14), for instance, a boy with a soft and girlish character, regularly cried in our presence:

> The other boys beat me up time and again. I can't handle it anymore. They always steal my money too. Yes, they always take me as their victim, because they know that I am too coward to fight back. I just don't know how to fight. They think I am a wimp.

The weaker street boys are also the victims of gang rapes and sexual abuse. Tom (19), an ex-street child in Cusco, recalled:

> There is a lot of sexual abuse on the street. The older ones abuse the younger ones. When I was young I always slept under the market stalls at San Pedro. But this market converted into a place for adult homosexuals and transvestites at night. They asked us for our arse and because we were young and needed money - most children said "okay". One day, while I was sleeping, a homosexual wanted to abuse me too. He was entering when I woke up and with my friend, we almost killed him; he was bleeding all over. Yes, in the street many strange things happen.

When asked to name the main perpetrators of violence on the streets, almost half of the street children pointed at the police, the municipal guards and other security forces. The relation that street children have with police on the streets is obviously confrontational and problematic. Children often complained that the police don't allow them to work, chase them, detain them, maltreat them, insult them or snatch their money. Peruvian law prohibits children from vending, begging or sleeping on the street and policemen are keen to implement at least this breach of law. The stories are full of anger, for example, Nina's (15, Lima):

> The *batida* [police raid] got me and a bunch of police men were pulling me in the car. They called me *puta* [whore] and *perra de mierda* [bitch of shit]. While in the car one of the officers touched between my legs: "let's see if this whore is still virgin", he said. "If you don't sleep with me I'll call your mother to tell her that you're a prostitute". So I said: "you dirty bastard, you're trying to manipulate me, *concha de tu madre* [motherfucker]". And he hit me. Pack! And again pack! That's how police are: dirty dogs who want to abuse us.

Police and street watchmen are not seen as protectors; street children generally talk about them as their biggest enemies. Bribery within the police system is also considered to be a major problem. The children report to have to pay 'fines' in order to be released. If they don't have the money, as is mostly the case, they are sent to the street to earn enough for their release. As Arturo (15) explained, 'first they detain you for stealing a car mirror, and then they say "'bring me 20 soles!", so you have to go and steal again a mirror, because how can you get this money otherwise?'.

Progressive exclusion from mainstream society is another consequence of street life. To be accepted by a street group and obtain protection and respect from other street children, the child has to adapt to street habits that are despised by society at large, such as poor vocabulary (slang), being tough/violent and using drugs. The more a child internalises these habits, the more excluded and disrespected by society he becomes, the more he is stigmatised and the more he becomes dependant on his social network on the streets. The child's chances to enter the formal labour market or educational system decrease once he enters the process, and slowly he is pushed into delinquency. This again deepens the social stigma of the street child and heightens the feelings of exclusion and marginalisation. Basically all street children in this research stated that they were being marginalised and often reflected on themselves as victims of society. The feeling of being excluded by others results in a low self-esteem and a lack of confidence, e.g. as expressed by Hector (15):

> I don't love myself, because I do many bad things. But my brain is already damaged. I take drugs, I have so many vices. Who wants to talk with a boy like me? I didn't study, I have no money. I have never done anything useful in life. I was never loved by someone. For me - my life is worth nothing.

Most of these children have gone to school at some point in their lives but dropped out before, or since, they started living on the streets. Among the children who don't live with their family only 16 % in Lima and 22 % in Cusco go to school. Of children working on the streets, but living with their relatives, these percentages are clearly much higher: respectively 77 and 86 %. The majority of street-living children in Lima and Cusco all seemed to agree though that school is very important and the only way of 'improving in life' and escaping the marginalised situation they are in. As Carman (14) said: 'Without school we can neither read, nor think properly. If you finish school you can present your papers at a job and they will accept you. Without papers you are nothing'. And Jherson (13) said: 'Someone who didn't study is not even contracted to wash dishes in a restaurant!' Livia (12), who lives in a rehabilitation centre and will start school soon: 'I want to finish my education, so I can become someone in life. I would like to be the first in my family with a real profession.'

However, in general, street children who attempt to return to school don't manage to stay there longer than a couple of days or weeks. The reasons for this low success rate are, among others, a lack of (mental, emotional and economic) support by adult wardens, a lack of discipline, peer pressure, drug addiction, low self-esteem, shame, discrimination in school, and poor quality education. Basic education in Peru is generally of poor quality. Salaries of teachers in Peru are extremely low, and teachers often have more than one job just to make ends meet. Their performance at school, with a responsibility for overcrowded classes, is often unsatisfactory. In general they don't have time to give special attention to problematic children; many street children feel misunderstood at school and become frustrated. After living on the streets and becoming adapted to street life, where timetables, strict rules and daily structure are basically absent, it is difficult to keep up with fixed school schedules. This is especially the case if the child still sleeps on the streets, or in unofficial hostels, while trying to attend school. Street children work till late at night or use drugs all night long, so they end up oversleeping, missing school, angering teachers and being suspended.

When questioned about their future, most street-living children expressed the wish in future not to live and to work on the streets. They all desired change and wished to 'become someone' in life and have a better working place. The dream of becoming a famous football player or musician 'and to have a good family, a piece of land, a house and a car, and all the things that I have never had', was often expressed by street children in Lima and Cusco. Besides a respected status and a good job, many children also expressed the wish to improve their family relations and reunite with their families. Statements like 'my dream is to go back to my family', to become 'a better person', and 'being someone in life', reflect the discomfort that most street children have regarding their current lives.

Contrary to the general opinion, which society has of street children, the wishes and aspirations of the street child are basically the same as the ones valued by society in general: having a family, having a formal job, finishing education, having a home, not using drugs, being respected and treated like everyone else. The children by and large hope to someday acquire a status respected by society, but most of them also admit making poor day-to-day decisions, which contradict these dreams, i.e. they cannot overcome their weaknesses.

4.6 Contrasts Between Street-Living and Street-Working Children

Numerous children from poor families are found within the informal sector. Among all street-working and street-living children included in the surveys, the most common activities (57 % in Lima and 54 % in Cusco) are selling (sweets, drinks, food, souvenirs, etc.) and working in services (26 and 24 %), including shoe shining (mostly in Lima), selling mobile phone calls (in Cusco), porting, washing cars/windscreens, arranging (collective) taxi passengers, operating weighing scales and assistant bus conductor. Other economic activities include playing music or singing on streets, in restaurants and in city buses (8 % in both cities, especially boys). Begging, stealing, street acrobatics (especially boys), recycling of waste material and prostitution were practised by only a few percentages of the street children. A considerable percentage (35 % in Lima and 28 % in Cusco) said to spend between 10 and 24 h on the street. Many of these children work at night, especially around cafés and discotheques, selling cigarettes and sweets to drunken men and women.

The majority of all street-working and street-living children (40 %) earn between 11 and 25 soles per day (between 3 and 6 euro); 33 % earn less and 25 % earn more. The data, which have been collected in the survey, make interesting reading. Although the self-reporting by the children may not be accurate or reliable, the results offer some indication of where the money goes: more on survival than on drugs or alcohol. Unlike street-living children, street-working children are generally strongly influenced by their parents, who mainly control their economic activities: they work to contribute to the household economy and hand over most of their money to their relatives. There is a gender difference, though, at least in Lima: 43 % of the girls and only 30 % of the boys give most of their money to parents or caretakers. Part of the difference may relate to the fact that there are many more street-living boys than girls. None of the girls mentioned spending most of the money on drugs or alcohol, while 4 % of the boys did, but boys, on an average also spend most of their money (41 %) on their own basic needs. School fees and necessities, often referred to as the benign reason why young children work, account for only 6 % (boys) and 8 % (girls). Boys, more than girls, spend some money on fashion articles such as mp3 players or mobile phones. Patterns in Cusco are slightly different. Among all children who earn money on the street, more than half of them hand it over to (one of) their parents. The remaining children spend most of their earnings on their own basic needs (24 %), on (fashion) clothes or (luxury) articles (4 %), on school articles (4 %), video games, pinball games or internet (2 %), drugs or alcohol (1 %) or they save their money (9 %).

As was argued before, there is a direct and strong relationship between street-working and street-living children; the line separating these groups is vague. Many street-living children started their 'street career' as street-working children (or even as street-roaming children). They share the same physical environment and therefore also many of the risks of this environment. Street-working children in Lima and Cusco are on the streets mainly for income generating reasons. They demarcate the difference with the street-living children in their involvement in illicit activities, begging, taking drugs, harassing girls, being out of school, etc. Whereas they actually tend to refer to them as *rateros, pirañas* or *maleados* (troublemakers), they regard themselves as being on the streets for 'good reasons', like helping their parents or earning money to pay their school fees. In a sense, public at large has a similar attitude. Children working on the streets are more socially accepted and tolerated than children living on the streets. Whilst street-living children are seen as an exception, street-working children are on the whole perceived as the norm in Peruvian society. Some street-working children nevertheless complained about how some passers-by consider them to be the 'same' as the 'bad *pirañas*', the street-living children, although they differentiate themselves quite deliberately. Lisa (14): 'I feel really sad if they call me *piraña*; they are the bad children, while we are good'.

It is mostly the parents of street-working children who decide on the time, the place and the methods of working. Although it is not always visible to outsiders, most young girls and boys (5–9 years old) perform their activities on the streets under supervision or accompaniment of adult relatives. Parents, in particular, coordinate the activity of the children and keep an eye on the children's safety and wellbeing from a distance. However, the majority of the street-working children and adolescents in Lima and Cusco—almost 40 %—are alone on the streets while they are working. Around one third spend their time on the streets with an adult relative, mostly a father or mother, and an almost equal number are on the streets with friends or minor relatives.

Rosada, a mother of three street-working children, admits that street work involves several dangers and that therefore her presence is necessary:

> I don't want my children to get in contact with bad children who steal and use drugs, the *pirañas*; I am afraid that my children will start to copy their behaviour. I prefer to take my children with me so I can keep an eye on them. In the market, there are many gangs. I am afraid my children will join the gangs or they will fight with them. If they are with me, they are safe.

As children grow older, the supervision by adults decreases, but whereas boys increasingly disassociate themselves from family members and increase their time with friends, girls start to spend less time with friends on the street, and increase their time with adults or relatives. There is also a major difference in social capital. Unlike street-living children, most street-working children ask adult relatives for help when they have a problem, or else friends and minor relatives. This shows that street-working children have a stronger social support network of family and friends they can rely on than street-living children.

The different locations where street-working children can be found in Lima and Cusco are the very same places where the street-living children hang around. Children selling handicrafts and souvenirs, or shoe shiners and postcard sellers, are normally found in the tourist and historic centres of the cities. Other popular places are commercial areas and entertainment centres, such as markets, shopping streets and areas with a high density of restaurants and bars catering for Peruvians. Big traffic intersections attract children that make a living with washing windscreens and acrobatic performances in front of traffic lights. Children who play music and ambulant candy sellers hang around bus stops and bus stations, where they jump from one bus to the other.

While street-living children generally spend up to 24 h on the street every day, the majority of street-working children spend between 4 and 9 h on the street. There is also a group of children that migrate by themselves from rural areas to the cities during weekends and school holidays to add to the family income.

Therefore, during school holidays and weekends many more children can be seen working on the streets. For example, Aurora (9) travels five hours by bus every weekend, with her younger brothers and sisters, from a small Quechua village to Cusco to sell *tostaditas* (dried seeds) on the pavements. Like Aurora, many of these children don't speak Spanish well, often don't know the city and lack a social network in the city. Therefore they are a highly vulnerable group for abuses by passers-by, street gangs and street-living children. They also run the risk to be negatively influenced by street-living children or end up staying alone in the city, especially if conditions at home are not good.

As stated before, one of the main differences between street-working and street-living children is the contact with the family. Street-working children generally maintain close ties with adult family members and live at home. Indeed, the majority (74 %) of street-working children in Lima and Cusco claim to see their relatives every day. It is either the entire nuclear family or the mother that children see the most. Even more importantly, as a marker between the two groups, when asked which place street-working children prefer to frequent, most street-working children mentioned their parent's house (34 % in Lima and 26 % in Cusco), the street (32 % in Lima and 29 % in Cusco) and their school (25 % in Lima and 37 % in Cusco). Very few street-living children mentioned their parent's house or school as their favourite places, probably due to the family problems they have experienced in the past.

The working children were asked about the reasons for their involvement in street work. The three most common answers were: because one of the parents told the child to do so, because the child has to earn money for his or her basic needs, or because the child wants or needs to help his or her family. The answers are overlapping; a child could often not remember if parents had instructed him, if he decided himself, or if it was simply necessary to provide for basic needs. Reasons for working are mostly a combination of the parents asking children to help and the child feeling the responsibility to contribute to the survival strategy of the family. Because parents often have insufficient resources to meet household needs for food and services such as healthcare and education, they will extend the family's labour time by sending the children to the streets to work.[2]

The restricted formal labour market coerces parents and their children into informal jobs where low earnings and harassment are the rule rather than the exception, as for example in the case of Mary, a single mother of six children, ranging from 3 to 15 years old and living in Cusco, who had tried to earn her living as an ambulant street vendor. For women like her, recurrent merchandise seizure implies starting all over again, with the possible consequence of feeling 'forced' to make instrumental use of their children: 'I used to sell underwear

[2] Not being able to sustain the household with the parental income can have various reasons, as Ensing (2008: 54) illustrates: 'lack of (well paid) employment for the parent(s), single parent families as a result of divorce, disease or death, a large number of children per household, high costs for basic services such as healthcare or education, and poor management of family money due to alcoholism or other problems'.

around the San Pedro market, but these 'monkeys' [police] were always harassing me. They are corrupt. Several times they took away my merchandise. They say that I am not allowed to sell on the street but how can I pay a fixed market stall?'. Mary explained that her children run fewer risks of being caught by the police, because they run faster and don't have valuable merchandise to lose. But also, children, she argues, are more accepted in low informal street jobs than adults. Her son Michael (7), who washes windscreens with his 3 brothers and sister at a big traffic intersection every day, continued his mother's story:

> It is hard to earn a living. Sometimes there is no food and we have to enter the restaurants to beg for food. Because they [the police] didn't let our mother do her work, we have to help her. There was no money left to buy us food or to pay my tuition fee, so we said "Mama, we will help you". That was one month ago, after the last time mother lost her stock of underwear.

Besides economic factors, the reasons for children to work are also often related to existing Andean traditional norms that see child work as part of children's socialisation process. For instance, various mothers and fathers of working children justified their children's work as a way for their children to learn how to be independent and responsible. They argued that helping with income generation teaches the children useful skills in life and makes them value their belongings. Nora, a single mother of five children, who all work as street vendors on the main square in Cusco, commented: 'Look, I am a single mother; what will they do if I die tomorrow? My children have to know how to earn their own money and how to survive. So it's necessary that they learn how to use their hands and be independent.'

It is a moot question whether it is a 'cultural tradition' as such, since many Andean families have modernised their tradition, particularly when they had the means to do so. In addition, 'culture' has a composite meaning; it is commitment to values and meaning as well as actually living practice. In the latter sense, culture is what people actually do and the so-called (Andean) culture is often a discursive explanation for what one is doing, a justification of one's behaviour, in disregard of what other people originating from a similar background, are doing. Behaviour then is probably influenced more by survival strategies than by a normative respect for ancient rules. Economic necessities set people on the move, opting out of their traditional habitat.

Entire families, and sometimes children on their own, migrate from the countryside to the cities to work and in search of better educational services. Many of them get stuck on the trail towards a better life. A reference to 'Andean culture' is less confrontational than a political analysis of injustice in society, an analysis which, at their level of abstraction, many people are acutely aware of. What mothers like Nora are actually saying is: 'Look, since we do not have access to good education, since we cannot manage to survive and since our children, unlike many other children, later on will have to work at the lower end of the labour market, it is practical to get them involved in work practice at an early age'. It is a rational response to the hard facts of life.

In comparison with the street-living children, school attendance of street-working children is relatively high. The great majority of them is enrolled or has finished education: 77 % in Lima and 86 % in Cusco of the street-working children who live with their family goes to school. Others have never been to school or they have dropped out. When asked why they have dropped out, by and large equal numbers mentioned the long working hours, the cost of education and the dislike for school. Having to work long hours on the streets is not only exhausting, but also reduces the number of hours at school or the time spent on completing homework, which can result in a definite school dropout. Although school attendance is fairly high among street-working children, many of them are poor performers and have an educational level below the level that corresponds with their age. Exhaustion is one factor. Habituation to a different lifestyle is a less tangible factor. Once a child becomes accustomed to earning money, he/she is likely to spend increasingly longer hours on the streets and the motivation to do well at school will suffer.

A large percentage of street-working children does encounter problems on the streets: 44 % in Lima and 32 % in Cusco expressed feeling unsafe. They refer to hazards such as the traffic doldrums and traffic accidents, pollution, violent passers-by and drunken men, verbal and physical violence, gang members, thieves, drug users, and, last but not least, police harassment. Similar to street-living children, the majority of street-working children accuse police and security forces as the main disturbers on the streets. Hazards are more likely in some of the areas, particularly in the outskirts of Lima. In Cusco the historic centre was considered to be the most unsafe neighbourhood. This is remarkable since this is also the area with most security forces. On the other hand, this could also be the actual reason for feeling unsafe: 40 % of the street-working children in Cusco consider police to form the major problem on the street.

Generally, boys feel safer on the streets than girls. More girls than boys experience sexual intimidation on the streets, while more boys experience physical violence and health problems and tiredness, mainly related to heavy jobs. Carla (9), who sells handmade hats on the *Plaza de Armas* in Cusco at night, commented:

> Yes, working on the street is dangerous. I know some girls who have been raped by tourists. And it also happened sometimes to me and my sister, almost. We always go to that dark alley to pee and it happens sometimes that some of the boys that hang around here follow us and ask us to be with them. But I always run away if I see them.

Thus, although most activities carried out by street-working children are seemingly harmless and relatively easy, the working conditions in which these activities are performed put the wellbeing, health and morals of the children at risk. Unexpectedly, feelings of safety decrease as children get older. This might be related to the fact that older children are less frequently accompanied by adult relatives, but also perhaps because older children are treated as adults, considerably harsher and more unforgiving than ways in which younger children are approached. Also, children who work with (one of) their parents on the street, claim to feel safer and happier, especially if the parent has a registered selling place on the street.

Yet, children who work on the streets run the risk of going off-track and becoming involved in even more hazardous and unacceptable forms of child labour, namely in unconditionally hazardous forms of child labour such as prostitution and drug trafficking. Street work in a malicious and violent street environment, especially if parental supervision is lacking, can damage the socialisation process of young children to such an extent that street work can result in a permanent stay on the streets and even worse working conditions. Once a street-working child starts to live on the streets permanently, working conditions worsen and he/she will encounter more hazards such as violence, sexual abuse, drug addiction, health problems, social exclusion and the lack of education.

References

Alarcón, W. (1994). *Ser niño. Una nueva mirada de la infancia en el Perú*. Lima: UNICEF-IEP.

Bourdillon, M., Levison, D., Myers, W., & White, B. (2010). *Rights and wrongs of children's work*. New Brunswick: Rutgers University Press.

Ennew, J. (1995). Outside childhood. Street children's rights. In: B. Franklin (Ed.), *The handbook of children's rights*. London: Routledge.

Ensing, A. (2008). *Child labour in the urban sectors of Peru*. Amsterdam: IREWOC.

Gigengack, R. (1998). De biodiversiteit van asfaltjungles: Straatkinderen in Mexico en Peru in een vergelijkend perspectief. In A. Gevers (Ed.), *Uit de Zevende*. Amsterdam: Het Spinhuis.

Gigengack, R. (2006). *Young, damned and banda. The world of young street people in Mexico City, 1990–1997*. Amsterdam: Amsterdam School for Social Science Research.

Mayuntupa, R. C. (2006). *La realidad sobre los niños, niñas y adolescentes en situación de calle*. Lima: CEDRO.

Panter-Brick, C. (2002). Street children, human rights, and public health: A critique and future directions. *Annual Review of Anthropology, 31*, 147–171.

Rizzini, I. & Butler, U. M. (2003). Life trajectories of children and adolescents living on the streets of Rio de Janeiro. *Children, Youth and Environments, 13*(1), 182–201.

Ruddick, S. (1996). *Young and homeless in Hollywood: Mapping social identities*. London: Routledge Press.

Visano, L. (1990). The socialization of street children: The development and transformation of identities. *Sociological Studies of Child Development, 3*, 139–161.

Woan, J., Lin, J., & Auerswald, C. (2013). The health status of street children and youth in low- and middle-income countries: A systematic review of the literature. *Journal of Adolescent Health, 30*, 1–8.

Wolch, J., & Rowe, S. (1993). Mobility paths of the urban homeless. *City and Society, 6*, 115–140.

Wolseth, J. (2010). Learning on the streets: Peer socialization in adverse environments. In D. Lancy (Ed.), *The anthropology of learning in childhood*. Walnut Creek: AltaMira Press.

Chapter 5
Street Child Interventions and Policies

The insight information on child street life will enrich the discussion on best practices. Policies relate to the legal framework, to the financial constraints and to the different vision and strategy which national authorities and NGO's have. The strict regime in children's home and the open-door shelters which accommodate the innate longing for freedom of these children are the two extremes. A soft approach, with the freedom and agency of street children in mind, unfortunately helps to facilitate self-destructive behaviour and leaves children where they are, generally for no reason of their own, at the margins of society. In exchange for love, respect and care, children may accept restrictions on their freedom.

The analysis of the background, the hazards and the aspirations of street-living children (and street-working children) provides us with a handle to assess policies. The literature on policies remains thin: 'policy-approaches have not made significant advances, as reactive, protective and rights-based models dominated the policy landscape around the world' (Thomas de Benitez 2011: 38). The three approaches (also: correctional/reactive, rehabilitative/protective and child-rights based) conceptualize the essence of the street child differently: as defiant, upsetting the social order, as a victim with deficient conditions of home life or as young persons who have rights to an autonomous living and whose rights have been denied. In the light of our previous analysis, the emphasis will be on the street child as a victim and on the need for protective measures.

Firstly, the role of the national and local government in protecting children will be discussed, including the legal framework of child protection in Peru. In particular, police attitude towards street children and attempts to 'remove' them from the streets, and lock them up, will be covered, before turning to a discussion on the services of non-governmental and welfare organisations that aim to improve the situation of street-living children. Particularly the positive and negative effects of their interventions on street-living children will be examined.

G.K. Lieten and T. Strehl, *Child Street Life*, SpringerBriefs in Well-Being and Quality of Life Research 15, DOI 10.1007/978-3-319-11722-5_5

5.1 Government and Non-government Approaches

Although the government of Peru has enacted several national laws in accordance with international conventions to protect children and adolescents, not much attention is paid to the specific situation of street children. The Convention on the Rights of the Child (United Nations 1989), which was signed by Peru in 1990, states in Article 20: 'A child temporarily or permanently deprived of his or her family environment … shall be entitled to special protection and assistance provided by the State'. Another agreement signed in 2002 is ILO Convention 182, which focuses on the worst forms of child labour. Members are obligated to 'take immediate and effective measures to secure the prohibition and elimination of the worst forms of child labour as a matter of urgency'. Hazardous forms of child labour, as defined in Recommendation 190, include all forms of abuses and work carried out in dangerous locations and in an unhealthy environment, including prostitution and drug trafficking.

Various national laws are in place. Particularly the Code of Children and Adolescents of 1993 established a set of norms to ensure the wellbeing of children. It includes the right to freedom, the right to live in a healthy environment, the right to grow up in an adequate familial environment, and so forth. The Ministry of Women and Social Development (MIMDES) is held responsible for the programmes, but in reality, priorities are missing and in recent years, successful programmes have been cut to size. The once successful street educator programme, initiated in 1993 by MIMDES, with about 300 street educators all over Peru, has been dramatically reduced since 2005. Officially, many programmes exist, such as 'Projoven', a programme that facilitates the entrance into the labour market for adolescents with limited possibilities, but as Thomas de Benitez (2003) argues, they are good examples of a broad-based initiative that includes street children in theory and in planning, but excludes them in practice. Broad-based programmes aim at 'poor youth' in general, and are likely to find street-based children too rebellious, aggressive and unskilled. Therefore street children are automatically de-selected; poor children from less violent, turbulent and neglectful homes are emotionally, cognitively and even physically better prepared for training.

The presence of street-working and street-living children is seen as a threat to public order and safety by the local governments. The 2004 Begging Bill (Law 28190: *Ley que Protege a los Menores de Edad de la Mendicidad*), many observers feel, has been 'misused' by police officers and authorities to remove street children from the streets and lock them up, as part of their policy of 'social cleansing'. Street vendors and street children are often treated like delinquents by the municipal agents and removed or banned from the city's streets. With this policy, street children are being pushed to areas outside the city centre, making them 'invisible' to tourists and local policy makers. Unannounced and violent police raids (*batidas*) are a common method to clear the streets from vendors, street children and prostitutes. The story by Ramon (14, Cusco) is not uncommon in Cusco's and Lima's street scene:

> One day we were walking on the sidewalk towards Plaza de Armas. Then there was a *batida*. Pack! Pack! Someone hit me on my back. It was one of the *monos* (monkeys, other word used for police). They loaded us all in their truck and took us to the *comisaría* (police station). One of the agents called us '*terokaleros, rateros*'. I asked him 'why?' and they accused us of robbing a tourist. If something happens, if some purse is stolen, they will always point at us.

During 'street-sweeping campaigns' children without adult supervision or street vending, are forced into a pick-up truck and brought to the local police station. At the police station they have to wait for a family member to pick them up. In case relatives can't be contacted or are not willing to come, the child or adolescent is transferred to special 'prevention centres', where they stay until a juvenile judge decides on further measures, i.e. mostly a transfer to one of the children's homes or a juvenile reformatory, often called '*la correcional*'. The police officers communicate with the children in an authoritarian and abusive manner. Within the *preventivos* or police stations, no special attention is given to the children's physical or psychological wellbeing, even though many children struggle with traumatic experiences and extreme backgrounds. Street child educators are critical of the centres. An educator in a children's home in Lima commented: 'They put all kinds of children together; delinquents with abused children and street children. The children negatively influence each other, i.e. motivating each other to turn to the streets after release. Police staff acts in an authoritarian and violent way, causing even more distrust and anger in the already psychologically damaged children'. After being detained in the *preventivo,* police station or juvenile reformatory, most street children, since no attention has been paid to their problems, very soon return to the structural circumstances of poverty and exclusion which led them to offend in the first place.

As a result of police repression and violence towards street children in the city centres, the children tend to move to the marginal outskirts of the cities. They consequently have become less visible and are increasingly alienated from mainstream society, which makes them even more vulnerable and an easy target for child traffickers, drug dealers and child prostitution.

In Lima a wide range of organisations are actively working with street-living children. There is a sharp debate between these NGO's. Ideological hardliners range from *paternalistic*, i.e. considering street children as a helpless and abandoned generation that has to be cared for, through to *protagonist*ic, which perceives street children as independent 'little adults' with the agency to make their own decisions about good and bad. While the former approach runs the risk of facilitating street life (the children know exactly when and where to go for their daily meal), the latter overlooks the self-destructive behaviour of street children.

Most of these organisations depend on funds from abroad, usually from the USA or Europe. The main challenge to the organisations, which overrules the ideological differences, is to have their aims correspond with the wishes of the street children. Both sides NGO's and the street children- indeed work within a different logic. While the former generally aim for school attendance, drug rehabilitation and a reintegration into society, the latter search for fun, freedom, respect, belonging and day to day necessities such as food and clothes. The main services offered by these

NGOs include outreach programmes with street educators, basic needs provision, permanent shelters, day shelters, night shelters, reintegration programmes, family counselling and healthcare. The programmes are diverse but they all function within the established conventions. There is hardly any out-of-the-box approach.

A lack of coordination between different teams of street educators, results in an overload of visits to street children in Lima Centre and a scarcity of attention to street children in other parts of Lima. In Lima Centre, every street child is generally in contact with more than 10 different street educators, all from different organisations. The Conos and dangerous neighbourhoods such as Callao and La Parada are, for example, rarely covered by street educators. Apparently the popularity of Lima Centre and the infamy of other parts of Lima relate to the 'number game'. All street child organisations are financially dependent on foreign sponsors, who fine-tune their financial aid according to statistics and the number of street children reached. As one extension worker stated: 'To achieve a high "score" and receive more funding, many organisations focus on high density areas, such as Lima Centre'. The higher scores which NGOs prefer to report in their annual statements and publicity documents, are often polluted. In general, the term 'street children' attracts more attention and sympathy from outsiders than, for example, the term 'poor children'. As a result many projects claim to target or claim to include street children to attract funding and volunteers, even though they may have very few, if any, actual street children.

5.2 Children's Homes and Shelters

In Lima, seven NGOs run nine permanent children's homes and 2 day shelters for street children. Cusco has one children's home and one night shelter, called dormitory. In children's homes with a small number of residents, children live more in a family-like atmosphere, while in the bigger shelters the atmosphere is generally more chaotic, authoritarian and hostile. The dormitories attract a variety of children that have a special relation with the street: boys and girls, young children and adolescents, drug users and non-users, orphaned children and run-away children, temporary and permanent users. The heterogeneous population can have a bad influence on some of the residents (e.g. introduction of the innocent to drug-use by the addicted).

The positive aspects of these children's homes and shelters, as mentioned by the children we spoke to during our research, are mostly related to good facilities such as food, water and beds (61 %). Other positive aspects are friendships with other children in the institution (27 %); the fact that people who work in there treat the children well (21 %) and the recreational activities (16 %). On the other hand, the most negative aspect is the lack of freedom (38 %); followed by bad relations with the other children in the institution (14 %) and with the people who work in the institution (18 %).

Especially the activities and workshops that children's homes and shelters provide are very popular among the children. Another important aspect of children's homes, according to many children, is that staff-members give the residents the feeling that they are important and that they matter. Especially in smaller homes with more staff, children feel respected and cared for. In such family-like places where the interaction between the staff-members and children are frequent and respectful, children often express their love for the staff-members and feel at home there. In some of the bigger children's homes, sometimes educators won't even know a child's name and treat them as clients instead of important individuals. Children in these kinds of homes express a feeling of disrespect, abandonment and loneliness. Fights between children occur more frequently in the overcrowded homes that have few supervisors. Even (sexual) abuse between children was mentioned as a problem in these homes. Street children have complex histories and therefore demand a lot of personal attention. Having good friends and feeling accepted is an important motivation to stay in a home, while fights and abusive relationships with other residents are reasons for a child to want to leave.

Typically, the majority of the street child population in Lima and Cusco has had the experience of living in one or more institutions at some point. A difference between the shelter and a children's home, as mentioned by the children, is that the shelter allows them to walk in and out as they want, but that in a children's home they feel locked up. Gustavo (15) gives this opinion on a night shelter in Cusco:

This is one of the few shelters where they respect us; they don't ask us to be a different person like they do in the children's home. Here I can come and go whenever I want.

Kevin (16):

> The problem is that I was used to street life. In the children's home they wanted me to change everything that I was used to. I only heard "you're not allowed to do this; you're not allowed to do that". They tried to discipline us. They punished us for everything. Well, then the choice for freedom is easily made.

Thus, street children expressed the need for a safe and warm place, but without losing all their freedom. The urge for freedom is the bottom line of street life. Street children are in general very much imbedded socially, culturally and economically in street life and their ties with the street will not be broken from one day to the next. The facilities children's homes are attractive, but the children don't stay put for long, move out into the street again and ultimately loose hope of ever leaving street life again. 'I simply can't get used to it', was the most often heard response. Often the most drug addicted children were the ones who had lost all hope in street child programmes and institutions. They mentioned an unwillingness to give up their friends, freedom and drugs for a life bound by rules and punishment, referring to bad experiences they had in the past.

All children's homes and shelters in Lima and Cusco claim to have 'semi-open doors': children enter the centre voluntarily, but if a child decides to stay, he/she has to follow the rules, has to go to school, and has to eat and sleep there. In practice, however, the meaning of semi-open varies; in some shelters the door is literally open and children can enter and exit whenever they want. They usually have a *regulacionista* approach.

An example of the *regulacionista* approach is a dormitory in Cusco that is only open during evening and night time. The mission of the dormitory is, according to one of their staff members, to improve the conditions under which children are made to work and 'to provide a shelter for the night and an informal space where they can learn in a pleasant rhythm and at the right moment'. This philosophy implies that a child should never be forced to do anything, like going to school, but that the wish to do something should first come from the child. At the beginning of a school year many children enrol in school, but within the first month the majority drops out. Although many factors can be blamed for this, as was noted earlier, various staff-members of other NGOs blame the dormitory's policy of 'voluntarism' for the dropout rates. An ex-educator from the dormitory clarified the problem as follows: 'You cannot always expect that children can make their own decisions. Neither should it be only the educator that decides for them. I think the problem of the method is, although the children should be free in their decisions, they also need someone who helps and guides them in making the right decisions'.

It is important to note that the open-door strategy of the dormitory is successful in attracting vulnerable street children who would never endure the strict rules of closed institutions. Without the dormitory these children would be at the mercy of sleeping on the street. Through easy accessibility and informal assistance the dormitory reaches an extremely marginalised street child population. It works very well as a practical approach, but when the ideology of agency comes in, tactical approaches are turned into strategy. Agency as a romantic notion of the wilful and resourceful child functions as argument for non-interference and many NGO's running the dormitories tend to regard the drop-outs as collateral damage. Their ideological stand on the agency of street children neglects to acknowledge the self-destructive behaviour of street children, like drug addiction, and their lack of socialised discipline as a major problem. It also negates the receptive mind of vulnerable children. Even children who had been placed in institutions and who had never lived on the streets before (e.g. abandoned or orphaned children) can become tempted by the stories they hear and sometimes decide to run away from the protective children's home to the 'open and free' dormitory. Once they start sleeping at the dormitory they come into contact with (drug-using and delinquent) street children and start to copy their behaviour. Because the shelter is closed during the daytime the children are 'forced' to spend their days outdoors, where they become accustomed to street life and how to earn their own money. Unqualified open access can thus stimulate the wrong kind of child agency.

The Cusco children's home, which we shall refer to as *Oasis*, is a good example of a semi-open access institution with a traditional approach, i.e. based on guidance and discipline rather than on freedom and agency. In the words of the Oasis director:

> These boys are too young to make decisions on right or wrong. They have a spoiled view on society, because they come from broken families with violence and alcoholism. Most of them have survived in harsh conditions on the street; they have been exploited and violated. The elder ones are addicted to drugs and alcohol; some were even involved in the sex industry. How can you accept their self-destructive decisions? First they have to rehabilitate; that needs a lot of strength and strict rules.

NGO's (and government institutions) are facing a serious dilemma. Strict rules, especially when under the tutelage of a religious dogma, make it hard for children to adapt. Hence, most children at Oasis are aged 8–12 years. There are few adolescents because many children fail to adapt to life with many rules and regulations and to the teaching of spiritual and moral values of the bible. Adolescents often cannot withstand the attraction of street life and 'to feel free again and be independent'. According to the director, 'in street life all the rules of mainstream society are broken and therefore the children can't get used to the rules we have here'. The lack of freedom is indeed most often mentioned as a reason for children to run away from Oasis. The longing for an unconstrained life on the street in combination with malfunctioning homes and abusive staff make it an uphill struggle, both for the staff and for the children.

Despite the high dropout rates for reasons described above, there are in fact also some very successful outcomes. An example is Sharon (16), who has been living in Oasis with her younger sister since she was 13 years old. Sharon recalled: 'It was difficult for me to adjust to this new life after what I was used to on the street'. Several times she went back to the street where she feels free, without rules. She described the constant dilemmas and also the attraction of Oasis as a safe and secure place, which ultimately withstood the enticement which street life offered:

> In the end I always returned to Oasis, because here it's better; you don't have to fight to survive. They give you food at fixed times, they give you love, they help you with your career and we get everything we need. And in the street, who is going to help you if you're sick? You can only endure. Who is going to help you? Nobody!'

Most homes with 'open doors', such as the dormitory in Cusco, close during daytime. Children have a different logic. They would like the homes to be at their disposal whenever they want and however they want; they criticised the limited opening hours of the dormitory and mentioned that it's hard to escape delinquency and drug abuse if you're forced to spend your days on the street. Carlos explained that hanging around on the streets led him to use drugs: 'My friends will push me to use and anyway, what else should I do the whole day?' It is hard for most children to change their lifestyle if they have no safe and welcoming place to turn to during the daytime, 'something like a home'.

'Something like a home', that is what the children have high in their expectations. During the daytime street children disperse in small groups across the city, but at night the dormitory is a meeting place for many of them. During group activities, such as games and football, they build up new friendships and develop feelings of solidarity. Besides the friendship, care and love the children receive from the educators they also stress the fact that they need someone who corrects them and helps them to keep on the right path. Many children felt that they 'really need and appreciate' this help from the educators, but like the institutions with their different strategies, they also are caught in a dilemma. Hector (16), for example, explained that he prefers to sleep in the dormitory, rather than at home or in the street, as he sometimes does. Like many children, Hector values the psychological assistance in particular but still tries to escape the waist jacket:

> We need psychological assistance to learn more about life. When we see him [staff member of the dormitory] in the street sometimes I quickly hide; I think "oh, this guy again comes to bother me". I feel like he's wasting my time. But slowly I'm learning from him and now I know that I'll not even reach my twentieth birthday if I continue like this. You know, it's so difficult to quit drugs, because it really dominates you, it's like you're trapped. You want to leave and leave, but the desire to take drugs always enters your mind. I cannot quit alone. I really need the educators' help.

Many street children said to prefer sleeping at the dormitory, rather than at a children's home, because 'here you are free and you can come and go whenever you want'. It is a mid-way station between getting off the street and remaining on the street. They can choose according to their convenience. A considerable number of street children alternates between spending the night at the dormitory and spending the night in a cheap hostel or in the street. They are constantly struggling between making the 'good choice' of sleeping at the dormitory or giving way to their desire for drugs. Hostel rooms are places where the children can sleep with their boyfriends of girlfriends and where they can 'get high on *terokal* all night long'. Hector explained: 'If I have money I prefer to sleep in a hostel, because that's the only place where they let you in [with drugs], as long as you pay the room'. When they don't have money they are likely to sleep in the streets, 'and because you are already so high you won't even feel the cold'. It is one of the many examples which indicate that children are shopping at different windows of opportunity and that outreach programmes operate within a continuous dilemma: minimizing the rules and obligations and thereby draw in more street children for basic supportive services or introduce a more disciplinary and pedagogical approach and alienate a chunk of the street children.

5.3 Different Approaches

It is important to gauge the assessment by the street children of the services provided. Many homes, keeping their ideology of agency in mind, have procedures to do this, but practice is frustrating, as we witnessed during two child participative meetings in one of the shelters. The children appeared to be unwilling to participate or didn't cooperate at all. Afterwards the children present stated that these kinds of meetings were boring and school-like or that they didn't know what to say. When we asked concretely what they appreciated or disliked about a specific children's home they lived in or had lived in, their answers were often clear.

The following answers were most commonly mentioned during informal conversations, group discussions and written assignments. They said to appreciate the activities and workshops, the good social relationships (with friends and with the educators), the care, attention, love, respect, help, counselling and guidance of the educators and other staff-members, the good (health) facilities and the food. They dislike authoritarian and punitive treatment, boredom and violent and abusive relationships. Thus, interventions should search for a balance between different strategies, so as to not disrespect street children's identities and wishes, but simultaneously seeking long lasting improvements for their wellbeing.

Whereas the children's home appear to impose a very strict regime, treating the children with rigorous discipline, the open-door shelters keep the innate longing for freedom of these children in mind, and manage to attract the children to the survival facilities which they offer. The reverse side of the coin, however, is that it helps to facilitate self-destructive behaviour and leaves children where they are, generally for no reason of their own, at the margins of society.

In exchange for love, respect and care, children may accept restrictions on their freedom. Experiences elsewhere indicate that much is to be gained by developing long-term packages of social protection and support (Thomas de Benitez 2011: 41). Such packages should take account of the child's voices and identities, should be cross-sectorial and should include support for the families and for institutional improvement in the communities.

References

Thomas de Benitez, S. (2003). Approaches to reducing poverty and conflict in an urban age: The case of homeless street children. In B. A. Ruble, et al. (Eds.), *Youth explosion in developing world cities. Approaches to reducing poverty and conflict in an urban age* (pp. 107–126). Washington, DC: Woodrow Wilson International Center for Scholars.

Thomas de Benitez, S. (2011). *State of the world's street children: Research*. London: Consortium of Street Children.

United Nations. (1989). *Convention on the rights of the child*. Available from http://www.hrweb.org/legal/child.html; http://www.unhchr.ch/html/menu3/b/k2crc.htm.

Chapter 6
Conclusions and Recommendations

A distinction has been made between children in the street and children of the street, or in other words street-working and street-living children. This research has confirmed that group boundaries are fluid, definitions overlap and children can move easily between categories. Yet, for analytical purposes, the distinction remains valid. Street children are embedded in a transition process, at the risk of moving from a street-roaming child to a street-working child and ultimately to a street-living child.

Studies focussing on the street-living child only, and highlighting their resilience and autonomy, fail to notice that children have landed up there by circumstances beyond their will. Poverty in itself doesn't drive children to the streets. Recent rural-urban migration due to chronic impoverishment is a strong independent predictor; single-parented families and reconstructed families are associated factors. In many children's accounts not the lack of money, but non-material factors, such as aggressive family relationships, the lack of communication and love, or the excessive parental authority, were fundamental in their final decision to leave the house. The street child is an integral aspect of the poverty hatchet. They belong to the colossal redundant and impoverished population, redundant in the countryside and marginalised in the cities. The discussion on child rights and on appropriate programmes needs to focus at that level.

The transformation from home-life to street-life is a complex process, with multiple push- and pull-factors in each individual case. The push-factors are negative features within the child's household, including domestic violence, parental alcoholism, low family income or unstable family income, neglect and abuse, a poorly functioning school system, poorly educated parents, the loss of parent(s), violence and the absence of parents at home because they are out working all day. The pull factors are aspects of street life that children imagine to be better than their current situation. They include, among others, freedom from restrictions, friendship and love among (street) peers, opportunities to earn an income, the addiction to drugs, the gang culture in the neighbourhood and the attractive

G.K. Lieten and T. Strehl, *Child Street Life*, SpringerBriefs in Well-Being and Quality of Life Research 15, DOI 10.1007/978-3-319-11722-5_6

possibilities of entertainment in the city. Neglect or abuse, however, usually precedes the construction of a new embedment on the street. This research has established that street life derives from a much wider condition of injustice and poverty.

Another important explanation for the transition into living rough goes beyond the push and pull factors. Children from impoverished families in marginalised neighbourhoods tend to start working in the street at a young age. We have identified a relationship between such street related work and the permanent transfer of the child from home to the street. As they start spending a lot of time on the streets, children also start to compare advantages of street life with disadvantages of their home situation, with the possibility of finally, in a gradual process, replacing home ties with street ties. Whereas it is analytically important to distinguish the categories, overall they belong to the category of street children and children on the street run the risk of turning into children on the street.

Once children are living on the streets, they usually may exhibit the characteristics for which such trendy concepts as agency, participation and resilience have been introduced. These are concepts with a benign message: children under adversity need not be portrayed as victims but as inventive and may display creative coping strategies. They are ascribed with multiple strategies for making a living on the streets, ranging from real labour activities to illicit activities. Recent anthropological studies, usually within the 'agency' approach confirm that street life indeed need not be hell on earth, at least not for the most vocal and talkative street children. This study confirms that, contradictory to the stereotypical image of street-living children, a number of them in fact appear to have money to spend, especially in comparison with street-working children: they often buy food, candies and soft drinks; they regularly buy new fashionable clothes and sometimes they can even afford accommodation.

A representative sample, as this study has attempted, learns, however, that the often-quoted conclusion by Aptekar (1991; see e.g. Panter-Brick 2002: 161) that they are 'clearly without pathology', is off the mark. Practically all the children loathed the conditions they came from. In other words, they conceived themselves as victims of an unjust social system.

Although in general, the street-living children enjoyed various aspects of the roaming life they had, they also identified many negative aspects. They are confronted with multiple hazards such as violence, sexual abuse, drug addiction and health problems. Their problems, however, are particularly related to social exclusion and emotional needs. They lack the feeling of belonging to a family, of having someone who really cares about them and feel the constant discrimination and condemnation by society at large. The children often expressed the wish to grow up in a united and peaceful family, but felt this right now was not an option for them. They actually had wishes for a future which were akin to what any middle-class and well-protected child could hope for. All the children hope to someday acquire a status respected by society, although most of the children admit to making poor day-to-day decisions, which challenge these dreams. They often realize that even although they manage to pull through in the short-term, their long-run prospects are weak.

Pulling-through in the short-term is being facilitated by the many shelters they can fall back upon. In Lima and Cusco we observed the work of various street child organisations and services to identify the positive and negative effects they have on street children. The organisation's ideologies range from *paternalistic*, i.e. regarding street children as a helpless and lost generation that has to be cared for, to *protagonist*, an ideology that perceives street children as independent 'little adults' with the agency to make the right decisions. While the former approach runs the risk of making children too dependent on the services (welfare) and of imposing a strait-jacket, the latter overlooks the fatal attraction of street-life and the self-destructive short-term behaviour of street children.

Strategies of street child services can be roughly divided into the reactive, the protective and rights-based approach. While police mainly follow a reactive approach, i.e. street children are seen as delinquents who have to be corrected through imprisonment and punitive methods, most (governmental and) non-governmental programmes follow the protective and rights-based approach. Through street outreach programmes, day shelters, night shelters and semi-open children's homes, they try to rehabilitate them or to help them 'to negotiate adversity'.

The common outreach programmes, apart from bringing services to the children, generally also function as the first step to get to know the street children and build up relationships of trust with them. Day and night shelters, in which children are free to come and go whenever they like, have a similar function, but in addition they also offer immediate protection, recreational activities, a starting point for rehabilitation, healthcare, mediation in family contact and (alternative) education. Outreach and day/night shelters manage to reach street children who otherwise would not receive other types of aid. However, these services are generally ineffective in helping children leaving street life altogether. They actually (unintentionally) facilitate street life with freely available *asistencialismo* (welfare) programmes. Care workers sometimes give the agency of street children too much credit and overlook the self-destructive and spontaneous behaviour of street children.

If a child chooses to leave street life, as most street children have at some/several points in their lives, a return to the family very often is impossible or unpractical. Instead, he/she can enter a children's home. Despite their inner longing for a place they can call home, and people who will give them care, guidance, boundaries and support, relatively few children actually manage to stay in a children's home for very long. Once inside they miss the freedom of the street, their street friends and drugs. Street children are very much imbedded, socially, culturally and economically, in street life and their ties with the street cannot be broken from one day to the next. Success rates may be higher with children who have recently moved to the streets, who have not yet become heavily addicted to drugs, and who have not yet become inextricably tied to a social network, are also still more willing to be helped by street educators. The more drug-addicted and adapted a child is to street life, the harder it is to offer adequate help and get the child of the streets.

Appropriate policies require a combination of integrated interventions, considering the diversity within the category of street children and the various reasons landing them on the streets. Volpi (2002), in a World Bank study of best practices, came up with a dozen 'essential ingredients' for successful programs: reaching children where they are (in the street); individualized attention, trained professionals, physical and mental health care, proper educational provisions, a focus on welfare of and integration into the family, the involvement of the community; tailor-made services and outreach programs, children's participation, lobbying and advocacy efforts, coordination and integration of services; networking and institutional cooperation, etc. (see also Thomas de Benitez 2003).

Not a single specific recommendation by itself will offer a solution to the problems of street children; it should be a collective and coordinated approach. Street child programmes should not be limited to the provision of basic assistance only, to avoid dependency and *asistencialismo*, but they should focus on child development and freedom from abuse. A comprehensive approach in any case would require street child organisations to cooperate in a joint effort. NGO's should be aware that 'aid-shopping', i.e. children taking from every organisation what suits them best, is being stimulated in a setting where different services are offered to the children. Street-living children excel in turning (welfare) organisations into a tool within their social network.

Once children are living on the streets it becomes exceedingly difficult to get them off the street, because of habituation to street life, the peer pressure, the comradeship and the addiction to drugs. Investments in prevention will be more lucrative. Such programmes will be difficult to implement. For example, since many of the street children are first or second generation migrants, the rural-urban migration should be halted through poverty reduction and investments in rural education. Also in the marginal outskirts of the cities, poverty reduction and the improvement of living conditions should be a major concern. Financial aid for low-income families and free/inexpensive healthcare and education can prevent parents from making instrumental use of their children or sending them to work. To avoid mothers bringing their children with them to the streets while working, quality public child care centres should be established in the at-risk neighbourhoods of the cities. Child protection mechanisms are vital, i.e. at an early stage, children should be helped and removed from violent and abusive family situations.

Family involvement in the rehabilitation of a child can help children come to terms with their traumas. In general, street children are more motivated to get out of street life when their families are supportive and care about them. Therefore, much attention should be paid to re-establishing family contact and family counselling and family development, i.e. searching for solutions for socio-economic and emotional problems within the families' household.

It is thus important to have street educators out in the streets on a regular basis. Especially children in the first stages of street migration, with moderate and less incorporated drug consumption, should be identified as soon as possible. The more addicted and adapted a child is to drugs and street life, the harder it is to offer adequate help and get the child off the streets. One of the main difficulties for street child organisations is their dependence on foreign donors, who (in most cases) are foremost interested in the numbers of street children reached. As a result, organisations compete for the children's attention instead of cooperating and focussing on quality and prevent street children.

Children off- and on the street encounter various forms of police violence and their children's rights are frequently violated. More control within the police system is essential to prevent the violent, corrupt and offensive methods used towards street children. Police staff at all levels should be trained on children's rights and the specific situation of street children. The situation in the juvenile custody and detention centres of the police should also be improved and made more child-friendly.

It seems vital that street child organisations do not jumble up children with a variety of histories and characters; children with different profiles should be kept separate according to age, gender and reasons for being in the institution. Overcrowded children's homes with few and unqualified staff members don't seem to be able to give street children the much-needed love, care and personal attention. Every street child organisation should have enough trained educators and psychologists to give individual attention to the physical and mental health of every individual child. Every street child has its own history, needs, aspirations and skills and therefore every child needs its own tailor-made rehabilitation programme. When a street child returns to school, a proper (psychological) preparation and intensive tutorial support outside school is determinant for success. It is almost impossible for a child to maintain his new lifestyle, without drugs and attending school, while still roaming around with the same street friends.

The policy complexity is understood in different ways. A comprehensive way to summarize what must be done is the following. A child protection system works efficiently, Balachova et al. (2009: 38) conclude 'only if adequate laws and policies are in place, services for children and offending and non-offending parents are available and public awareness and community support are adequate'. It is a tall challenge for these factors to combine, but even then, one major element, the bottom line of all policies, is missing: the financial wherewithal and stage of economic development which will allow governments to intervene effectively, for despite the various claims to best practices, NGO's on their own remain a minor and dispersed social force.

References

Aptekar, L. (1991). Are Columbian street children neglected? *Anthropology of Education, 22*, 326–349.

Balachova, T., Bonner, B., & Levy, S. (2009). Street children in Russia: Steps to prevention. *International Journal of Social Welfare, 18*, 27–44.

Panter-Brick, C. (2002). Street children, human rights, and public health: A critique and future directions. *Annual Review of Anthropology, 31*, 147–171.

Thomas de Benitez, S. (2003). Approaches to reducing poverty and conflict in an urban age: The case of homeless street children. In B. A. Ruble, et al. (Eds.), *Youth explosion in developing world cities. Approaches to reducing poverty and conflict in an urban age* (pp. 107–126). Washington, DC: Woodrow Wilson International Center for Scholars.

Volpi, E. (2002). *Street children promising practices and approaches.* Washington, DC: The World Bank Working Papers (26388).

CPSIA information can be obtained at www.ICGtesting.com
Printed in the USA
LVOW05s2323311014

411472LV00003B/85/P

9 783319 117218